# Outstanding

## Teaching, Learning

## and Assessment

## The Handbook

## Robert Powell

Published by Robert Powell Publications Ltd
56 Stockton Lane
Stafford
ST17 0JS

First published August 2010
Reprinted 2010
© Robert Powell 2010

ISBN-13: 978 1 901841 35 9
ISBN-10: 1 901841 35 9

Version previously published as Personalised Learning in the Classroom 2006.

The Publishers would like to thank the following organisations and people for their help and contributions to this book:

Cutting Edge Publications; Inglehurst Junior School; John Murray Publishers; Network Continuum Publishers; Promethean; Michèle Deane; Gareth Jones; Coby McKeon; Maggie Pringle.

Thanks also to 1000s of outstanding teachers whose ideas and creativity have inspired the author over many years.

Editor: Pat Winfield
Designer: Neil Hawkins, ndesign

Printed in Great Britain by Cambrian Printers, Wales

# Contents

# Foreword

Most of the ideas in this handbook were published previously in an earlier book *Personalised Learning in the Classroom*, first published in 2006. That book had been re-printed twice and now another reprint was needed. I decided to make a number of small but significant changes before re-reprinting that included a change of title.

*Personalised Learning* was one of the buzzwords for a previous government and the term '*outstanding*' more accurately captures the current agenda for schools and colleges. The original handbook examined outstanding practice in the personalisation of teaching, learning and assessment so the ideas and techniques within each section apply equally to the new title.

There is also a stronger emphasis on principles in this later version of the book. I continue to work on teaching and learning with schools and colleges across the UK. The pressure to improve results in incessant and I am increasingly concerned with the number of leadership teams that resort to rigid lesson planning frameworks as the means to improving performance. I do not believe that this is the solution. Indeed, I am convinced that such approaches might have an unintended impact; moving poor teachers up the scales and outstanding ones down. The concept of agreed school- or college-wide principles as the basis for a policy on teaching, learning and assessment provides a rigorous framework for developing outstanding practice.

There are several changes to the original handbook – for example, details of new software are included – but essentially it is unchanged from the earlier version. There is no intention to deceive anyone into purchasing another copy of a previous book. Indeed, any reader who has purchased this book expecting an entirely new publication and feels misled should call the publisher's sales line with a proof of purchase and an immediate refund will be forthcoming.

*Robert Powell*

# Introduction

**The accolade of 'outstanding'**

In recent times, the term 'outstanding' has become increasingly significant in the world of Education. In England, the Ofsted framework for school and college inspection uses the term to denote a grade 1 category in its evaluation schedule and although no school or college is driven simply by a desire to achieve good inspection grades, there is no doubt that the accolade 'outstanding' is keenly sought by those involved.

The handbook concentrates on 'outstanding' practice and is divided into three sections on the principles and practice of teaching, learning and assessment. This is not to suggest that the headings represent three separate or independent activities or functions. Indeed, the opposite is true. All are interdependent and there will be many occasions when a particular activity has elements of all three in evidence, a true reflection of the complexity of classroom interaction. The handbook sets out principles that might form the basis for policy and then provides examples of what the principles might look like in practice.

**A framework based on the four- or five-part lesson**

The policy section is very brief, but it introduces an approach that needs some explanation. Each section begins with a set of 'principles': principles for teaching, principles for learning and principles for assessment. Outstanding classroom practice, as I will demonstrate later in the main body of the handbook, is hard to define but easy to recognise.

Ask students to describe outstanding lessons and nearly all will mention 'passion', 'variety' and 'creativity'. Yet many school and college leaders face a dilemma: in their hearts they will agree with their students on the issue of variety and creativity, but in their heads they keep coming back to the words rigour, attainment and inspection. Such concerns often lead to the introduction of a rigid framework for lesson planning. The four- or five-part lesson is one example of such a framework. All lessons must begin with a starter followed by an introductory phase. A deepening of understanding phase follows and then the lesson concludes with a plenary. This is a simplified version of a lesson plan used in thousands of schools and colleges.

Such rigid frameworks may have short-term benefits – where, for example, planning is poor or non-existent. But it is not, in my view, a formula that is going to develop 'outstanding' practice. The four- or five-part lesson is going to produce a conformity that resembles 'teaching by numbers', where most lessons look and feel the same and where passion, creativity and variety are conspicuous by their absence. This lesson structure works well for some teachers for some of the time, but it is a straitjacket that hinders and frustrates many good professionals. Teachers of Art and Design, for example, do not function with single lesson plans – they work in episodes of several lessons or even weeks and for them to be forced to have a starter and a plenary each lesson is nonsensical. This will be true for many others working in assignment-led courses where individual students may be working independently on a variety of tasks.

## A teaching, learning and assessment policy based on principles

This is why the concept of a teaching, learning and assessment policy based on *principles* is an attractive alternative. It provides rigour and accountability, allows monitoring and evaluation but also encourages passion, creativity and diversity of practice while supporting professional autonomy.

### How does it work?

It is a fairly straightforward process. Schools or colleges agree principles for outstanding teaching, for outstanding learning and for outstanding assessment. Examples of such principles are used in this handbook, but ideally principles will be discussed and agreed by the leadership and staff (and possibly students) of the individual institution.

These principles now become non-negotiable – they are the foundation for the policy on teaching, learning and assessment. Each team (department, year team, faculty) now identifies a range of strategies used by that team to meet each principle. All the best techniques and ideas are shared and then included in the 'how' section of a 'handbook of outstanding practice' for each team. So, the principle that all learners are clear on learning aims at the beginning of a lesson is non-negotiable. But in practice, one teacher shares aims on a flipchart displayed on the wall, another uses a visual map, another starts with a multimedia stimulus, another with a set of key words, and in Art students arrive and simply start work because the learning aims are clear from an earlier lesson and they have personal logs recording their progress.

The principles are non-negotiable but the practice is varied, creative, stimulating and engaging and takes into account the varied demands of different subjects. Furthermore, teachers are making decisions based on their preferences and professional judgements. Finally, the building of a team handbook of outstanding practice is a superb staff development process. The best ideas and techniques are recorded using a shared language and it becomes a manual that team members can consult in the planning of lessons.

## Principles in the handbook

While each section defines a number of key principles that, I believe, underpin outstanding practice, the majority of the handbook is devoted to the 'how' question. Most teachers will have come across policies that are no more than sound bites.

> *"Teaching should maximise the potential of all students."*
>
> *"Assessment should be used to identify the needs of learners."*
>
> *"Learning tasks should be differentiated."*
>
> *"Lesson objectives should be clear."*
>
> *"A variety of learning and teaching styles should be used."*

Such phrases will appear in the learning and teaching policies of most schools and colleges. In successful institutions, and those that are making year-on-year improvements in spite of the most challenging circumstances, it is highly likely that such phrases represent the reality of classroom life and are the basis for planning, review and reflection. Teachers and support staff understand the principles behind the policy statements – *why* they are important – and *how* they can be applied. However, where underachievement is widespread, the policy statements can become mere platitudes. Some teachers will not understand the principles behind the policy statements and fail to apply them. Some will understand the principles but not know *how* to apply them.

That is why each principle is followed with a range of examples of how it might be applied. The examples are not meant to be the definitive list – some of the ideas will have been used by readers for years, some will be welcome additions and some will be judged to be inappropriate for the subject, age group or ability of the class. Some will have other and better ideas or strategies that will serve to meet particular principles.

I hope, therefore, that school and college managers will use this handbook in the development of key principles to develop outstanding practice in the classroom, and that practitioners will use the ideas as a springboard for the development of other strategies and techniques to add to their handbooks of outstanding practice.

Most professionals in education accept key principles in a matter of minutes, but turning those principles into practice is the challenge. I hope that this handbook helps to do that.

Robert Powell

# *Outstanding...*

| Principle | The Challenge |
|---|---|
| **1.** Provide the classroom environment that allows individuals to flourish. | Individual students vary enormously in their levels of skill, confidence, motivation, willingness to contribute, learning styles and behaviour patterns. The challenge for teachers is to create a positive, safe and welcoming environment for learning and this can often be achieved through the use of clear, fair, consistent and public systems of classroom management. |
| **2.** Ensure that all students understand the learning aims and their link to prior learning. | If all students are to engage fully with the learning and to enjoy a sense of purpose and fulfilment then they need to be absolutely clear on what their learning aims are. The challenge for teachers is to communicate these aims to all, even to those who have difficulties in listening or reading. |
| **3.** Ensure that all students understand key vocabulary. | All subjects have sets of technical vocabulary that underpin the learning. For some students exposure to such terms is a source of anxiety, and the challenge for teachers is to help all learners to feel comfortable with the key words. |
| **4.** Ensure that all students are willing and able to participate. | In the better lessons, most students participate in speaking and in thinking. But not all students are motivated or confident enough to participate in this way. The challenge for teachers is to encourage widespread, engaging and anxiety-free participation. |
| **5.** Review, identify and celebrate learning, during and at the end of the lesson, to ensure that progress and success are recognised. | Success can become addictive and yet not all learners are always aware when they are making progress. The challenge for teachers is to ensure, through regular recapping and an end of lesson review or plenary, that all students recognise their progress in meeting the shared learning aims. |

# Teaching

# Climate and Ground rules

## Welcome

Strive to welcome students to lessons. Be at the door when they arrive (if you are fortunate to work mainly in one teaching base). Show some interest in them. Make them feel valued. Supervise their arrival with a smile.

## Be positive

Encourage students to participate by being positive when they ask or answer a question, offer an idea or an opinion. Offer praise when appropriate. Never use put-downs or sarcasm. Do not allow other students to ridicule or to use put-downs with each other.

## Celebrate

Try to ensure that students leave your class at the end with their heads held high. Celebrate the learning with all the students when real progress has been made.

## Start as you mean to go on

Rules for health and safety in a science laboratory, engineering workshop, swimming pool or gymnasium are often called 'ground rules' - procedures, rules, and ways of working that teachers insist students adopt during lesson time.

Ground rules will vary from teacher to teacher or department to department and will often be linked to the activity, the environment or the subject. There will also be differences for different age groups – teachers of post-16 students or adults will adopt ground rules that are appropriate for that audience. Some ground rules such as 'face the teacher', 'put your pens and pencils down' and 'no talking' while the teacher or another student is addressing the class are optional but widely used and often very successful. Other ground rules – such as never allowing ridicule or abuse in a classroom – should be universal.

## Procedures

Many teachers make use of rituals or procedures that bring a sense of order to classrooms, particularly to large classes. Remember, classrooms are often busy and complex environments where a variety of tasks and activities are being performed simultaneously. Such procedures can reduce stress and improve the atmosphere for effective learning. Teachers and students all benefit from such clear and consistent rituals:

- Book monitors putting away the resources.
- Book monitors from new class distributing books.
- A 'flipchart' monitor is putting up this lesson's learning aims sheet (see page 26).
- Arrivals are getting out exercise books or folders and entering the date and aims while they wait for the starter.
- If teachers are using a Promethean interactive whiteboard, instructions can scroll across the board as students arrive.

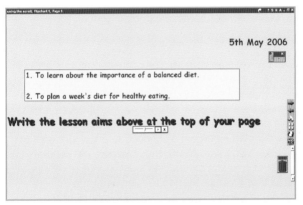

The blue text scrolls on this Promethean whiteboard
as the students arrive.

## Practical lessons and 'starters'

The change of lesson procedures set out above may vary in practical lessons. Many schools insist upon lesson 'starters', but in some practical lessons, for example during assignments in Art, Design and Technology or Engineering, students may know what they are doing and want to proceed without waiting for the teacher to 'start' the lesson. This is perfectly sensible and a good example of a 'rule' on lesson starters being guidance rather than 'set-in-concrete law'.

Classroom environment

# Seating and display

## Seating arrangements

Most experienced teachers will have experimented with the layout of tables in their classrooms. No single layout will be perfect for all occasions: rows of desks hinder movement; grouped tables inhibit individual study; boardroom styles discourage group work. Teachers will have their own preferences, and some will have little choice as they wander the corridors with their blue, plastic boxes.

The arrangement opposite – the 'cabaret' arrangement - is an ingenious layout that allows students and teacher to move between whole-class teaching, small group work and individual study without moving furniture, and movement around the room is also possible without barging and interference.

## Ground rules on seating

But it is advisable, for all sorts of reasons, to start with the ground rule that 'where students sit and whom they sit with is the decision of the teacher'. In schools this should be a whole-school rule supported at all levels. This does not mean that all teachers will have a strict seating plan – some may choose to allow students to sit where and with whom they please. That is fine because it is still the teacher's decision. But others will decide to arrange seating to support group activity, others to separate unhealthy relationships, others to provide peer support.

Such clear ground rules for seating are particularly important if teachers choose to make use of two of the techniques described in the handbook – Snowball (page 38) and Support Groups (pages 50 and 68). Both of these techniques require students to make use of small groups for short, focused activity, and being able to form those groups quickly and easily without furniture re-arrangement is vital if they are to be wholly effective.

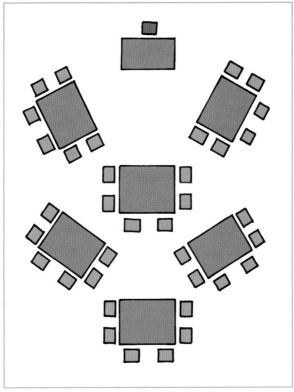

This 'cabaret' arrangement, from Philip Waterhouse's book *Classroom Management*, is one of a number of arrangements set out for consideration. More details in the Resources section on page 144.

## Display

Classrooms and workshops should be seen as 'places of learning'. They should be attractive to the eye but more importantly should act as a resource for both the teacher and the students. All kinds of use can be made of display:

1    The display of key words with images if possible.
2    The use of visual maps of the topic or unit.
3    The celebration of students' achievements and work on the display boards.
4    The display of models of good practice for students to study.
5    Visual access to information or stimulus from posters, photographs, maps, diagrams, models and artefacts.

Classroom environment

# Questioning and discussion

## Questioning and discussion

Low-level disruption in classrooms is often much harder to deal with than the high-profile cases of abuse and assault that can be dealt with through effective and clearly defined sanctions. Few teachers would want to seek support from middle or senior managers for minor indiscretions. Yet students who constantly shout out during questioning or discussion not only irritate teachers but also create an atmosphere where the more cautious or less confident students feel less disposed to participate. It is worth spending time, therefore, on the establishment of clear ground rules for this type of activity.

## Hands up

The simplest and most common strategy is to ask students to put up their hands when they wish to speak. It might seem patronising to include such an idea, but it is surprising how many teachers claim to adopt such a rule but fail to impose it. Once students learn that they can 'get away' with shouting out they will do it constantly. The rule, if appropriate, must be rigorously enforced. Every time an interruption happens, teachers must stop and remind the student(s) that such behaviour is discourteous.

## Whole-Class discussion: the Chair and Scribe

This system can work well. One of the students is asked to chair the discussion and another is the scribe. The Chair keeps eye contact with the student currently speaking while the Scribe catches the eyes of students who wish to speak and writes their names down. When one student finishes speaking, the scribe invites the next person from the list. These roles are shared out. What is very effective about this is that all are aware of the rules, and if anyone breaks this rule it is the Chair, another student, who reminds the offender. I have seen teachers choose the most disruptive student to chair the discussion. Once she/he keeps to the rule, others do as well.

## Numbering

Many years ago I was covering a lesson for an absent colleague. When I walked into this class a little late, some thirty 11-year-olds were seated in a circle while a girl with learning difficulties sat at the teacher's desk. She quite calmly instructed me to take a seat and asked me if I wanted a number. She explained that this was a weekly discussion lesson on the news and current affairs and that it was her turn to chair the discussion. Students who wished to speak were given a number and only spoke when the number was called.

I was given number 31. At one point I interrupted someone who had made a factual error on some aspect of the news and the Chair calmly told me not to interrupt and to put my hand up. When that student had finished she said, "Now, Mr Powell. Did you wish to say something?" I subsequently used this system for many years!

## Sweep

This is very much like the numbering system above and also makes use of a circle. But in the 'sweep', when one student finishes the person to the right then speaks and so on until everyone has had a turn. (This idea is from Philip Waterhouse's Classroom Management book – see Resources section on page 144.)

## Play the Joker

In this activity students are paired carefully in such a way that the most confident student partners the least confident, the second most confident with the second least confident and so on. It works well as a lesson starter for the learning of key technical vocabulary. Twenty key words are identified and displayed each week and at the beginning of the lesson the teacher asks one of the students to explain its meaning. If one of the less confident students is unable to answer, she/he can call out 'I'm playing my Joker' and her/his partner is given the chance to answer. It reduces the stress of the question/answer session and students enjoy this short, but stimulating activity.

My thanks are due to Michael McEnery, Senior Teacher responsible for ICT at St Michael's Grammar School in Lurgan, Co Armagh for this example.

# Use of groups

## Use of groups

Some teachers make good use of groups in their teaching and others are reluctant. There is no doubt that well organised and focused group work can be highly effective, but it is equally true that if clear ground rules are not in place and if the task lacks organisaton and focus then group work can be a skiver's charter.

## Record the name

One of the most commonly perceived problems with group work is the situation where groups of four students are asked to brainstorm a list of ideas, solutions or questions. In reality, one student does most of the work and three do very little. When the teacher praises the list produced by the group, the student who actually did the work feels aggrieved. This outcome can be avoided with the following strategy.

All groups appoint a Chair and a Scribe. The Chair's role is to ensure that the task is completed within the time allocated and the Scribe's role is to record the ideas. But the significant point is that for each idea or question listed, the Scribe *must record the name of the student who thought of it.* As the teacher patrols the class, prompting and supporting, the praise is given to the students who deserve it. *All students want their names on the list.*

| Discrimination | Whose idea? |
|---|---|
| Women's pay in equal jobs | Amanda |
| % of women in senior management | Karl |
| Maternity rights | Juan |

## Group contract sheet

Another way in which the work of groups can be more closely monitored is by the use of a contract sheet like the one following.

| Group Work Contract Sheet | | | |
|---|---|---|---|
| **Who** | **What** | **When by** | **Teacher signature** |
| Student A | The workhouse | Monday | *A. Teacher* |
| Student B | Sanitation in the slums | Monday | *A. Teacher* |
| Student C | Crime | Monday | *A. Teacher* |
| Student D | Disease and life expectancy | Monday | *A. Teacher* |

If, for example, the task is to record the living conditions of the poor in the slums of 19<sup>th</sup> century London, the individuals might decide to research:

    (a) the workhouse
    (b) sanitation
    (c) crime, and
    (d) disease and life expectancy.

These plans are recorded on an A5 record sheet and the teacher signs the 'contract' when she/he is happy with the plans. This ensures that each person in the group has a personal responsibility, and although the teacher will still have to monitor that individuals do what they are supposed to, it does provide a higher degree of control and focus for the work of the group.

## The Jigsaw

This activity is included because apart from it being a good example of differentiation, it also illustrates high-quality classroom management.

The purpose of the Jigsaw is for a small group of students to collaborate in the production of some kind of finished product that has a number of component parts. Each member of the group has responsibility for one of those parts, and when all have finished and the parts have been put together you have the finished article - thus the name 'jigsaw'. The groups must be formed so as to be balanced in terms of confidence or skills.

## Modern Languages example

In the example following there are 16 students in the class, divided into 4 groups. These might be called the 'home' groups. Each group is told it must produce an information pack on leisure activities for exchange students about to visit their town from abroad. Each pack must contain:

A   *A poster with images and words that informs visitors of what leisure activities are available in the area.*

B   *A letter, to the visitors, written in the foreign language, informing them of facilities they will find when they arrive and what they might or could do when they arrive (using future and conditional tenses).*

C   *A list of possible activities with the costs in euros for each activity.*

D   *An audiocassette where details of the leisure activities have been described in the foreign language.*

Each 'home' group decides which task will be done by which student – the teacher may judge Tasks B and D to be the most challenging, Task C to be of average challenge and Task A to be the least challenging. Students are allocated tasks accordingly.

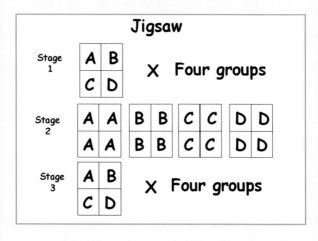

The differentiation strategy is that at this point all the Task A people from the four groups now meet in what may be called 'away' groups. Those allocated Tasks B, C and D do likewise, and the planning for these tasks goes on in each 'away' group compiled of students doing the same task. All students have to produce their own versions of the product they are allocated, but they do so with support from the others.

When they have finished, they all return to their 'home' groups, taking the component part they have completed with them. The jigsaw is complete. The Jigsaw supports individuals because:

1. All individuals have a real responsibility and a personal role.
2. No individuals can take over and dominate a group.
3. Questions come from the safety of the group.
4. Teachers can provide better support to a group doing the same than if all four members were doing different tasks.

## Mastery

One use of small groups that works well is an activity called *mastery*. The purpose is for small groups of students to raise the performance, knowledge or skills levels of its members through peer support or peer coaching. It works like this:

1. Form mixed ability groups ensuring a balance in terms of skills or confidence. Do not put all the most or least confident students together.
2. Agree the purpose of the task e.g. to revise the definitions or spellings of key words; to practise mental calculations.
3. Give the mastery groups time to revise this topic together (the amount of time will vary upon the situation or task).
4. Give the whole class a test on the agreed topic (e.g. 20 questions).
5. Give out the answers and ask each group to mark its own answers (requires trust!)
6. Ask each group to read out (or bring out on a piece of paper if confidentiality is important) the total score out of 80 (assuming 4 per group) for its group.
7. Celebrate achievement and set each group a target for improvement next time.
8. The only way a group can improve its score is through peer coaching.

As you would appreciate, the ground rules of this activity must be firmly established – no abuse!

# Visual maps

## The big picture and prior learning

It is important that learners are able to see the 'big picture' when beginning a new programme of work. This overall picture or map of the new learning may contain elements of prior learning, enabling students to make links between what they have done already and what is to come. Many of the exercises and activities included in the Review Learning section starting on page 50 can be used here as a starter to review and recap on prior learning.

## Visual maps

One of the best ways to provide the 'big picture' is through the use of visual maps. Visual mapping, model mapping or concept mapping as it is variously called, is very popular now with teachers from all phases. It does not require any particular technology to make it a valuable learning experience – some coloured pens and sheets of A3 paper are all some teachers and students need.

The visual map on the opposite page, however, was developed using The Visual Planner software *EyeWrite* (see page 80 and the resources section on page 144) and can be used by teachers or students for planning any kind of lesson, writing, report or presentation.

Mapping can be used for a variety of purposes: for the development of thinking skills; for memory; for formative assessment; for revision; for planning; for summarising. It can also be an extremely effective way for teachers to share the 'big picture' with students at the beginning of a course or unit of study.

In the example opposite, the teacher is showing students the major topics that will be covered in their Civil Rights course. The four key headings present a chronological approach beginning with Abraham Lincoln and ending with Martin Luther King. Each of the smaller 'branches' represents some of the issues that will be examined during the course. The software allows it to be sent to the students' PCs and they can add to or amend the headings for personal study.

Mapping provides a visual summary that helps students to locate the new topic in terms of existing knowledge, but it will also help them to 'navigate' the new topic in a way that the syllabus might not. Examination boards often present their syllabi in dense, closely typed documents that do little to help those with weaker literacy skills or those who perform better visually.

This will work in all phases and with the growth in the use of the web and of digital cameras, teams of teachers can collect and store a wide range of photographs or illustrations that can be used to map any topic visually.

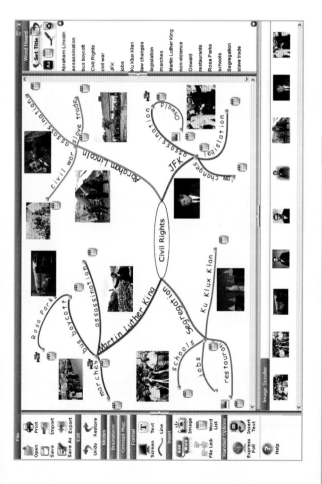

Understand learning aims

# Visual summaries

There are a number of ways in which visual summaries can be used.

Timelines in History are just one example where a series of dates or events are presented chronologically on the wall or on a poster and key words or images are added depicting the key ideas or issues that the teacher wishes to emphasise.

For example, the timeline opposite, once completed by the class, might be displayed in the classroom or used on an OHP or interactive whiteboard as the 'big picture' for a series of lessons on the Vietnam War.

## Interactive whiteboard

A visual or timeline approach will work brilliantly on an interactive whiteboard. The teacher can progressively build up a visual record of the learning that has taken place, saving the file for review at the beginning of the next lesson and updating again at the end, all with the active participation of the students. Students will be eager to annotate and amend the images or text on the screen and a final version can be printed out and distributed to the class whenever the teacher feels it is appropriate.

Visual summaries do not have to be chronological, of course, but can set out a range of visual stimuli to aid thinking or recall.

Such approaches can be used in other areas of the curriculum:

- The story of the rain cycle (Geography)
- Art through the ages (History of Art)
- The working of the heart (Science)
- Fuel systems (Engineering)
- Members of the family (Modern Languages)
- Healthy Eating (Food Technology, Health and Social Care)
- Civil Rights in the USA (R E, Citizenship, Sociology)
- Macbeth (English, Drama, Performing Arts)

**Understand learning aims**

- Fitness programmes (Physical Education, Sports Science)
- Hygiene (Catering, Hair and Beauty)
- Successful design (Art, Design and Technology)
- Composition (Music)
- Health and Safety (a variety of vocational subjects).

Such examples could be extended to include all subjects and all age groups from infants to adults. (See Learning logs on page 62.)

This map is displayed from the beginning of the topic. The teacher can begin by using the timeline to give a brief outline of the whole story with contributions from the class who may have some knowledge from reading or from films on the subject.

From Modern World History, by Ben Walsh. Reproduced by permission of John Murray

**Understand learning aims**

# Snippets to create interest

The opening pages of some novels have the reader engrossed even before the plot or characters have been introduced. The trailer to a film or video is designed to make viewers want to see more. In both situations the authors or producers offer tasty snippets and the purpose is to 'hook' the audience.

Teachers can do the same to great effect at the beginning of a new topic:

> *"We'll be finding out why Henry VIII ..."*

> *"How do you think we know that...? By the end of this... (topic/lesson) we'll be able to answer that question..."*

> *"What do you think happens if...?"*

> *"That is the answer. Let us see if we can work out what the question was."*

> *"You may not believe this, but..."*

> *"There is a real problem here. I wonder if anyone will be able to solve it by the end..."*

Indeed, some of the most interesting lessons will start with the teacher leaving the students wanting more.

The Royal Institute Lectures in Science, shown on television every year at Christmas, are one of the best examples of this strategy in action. The presenters never fail to stimulate their invited audience and the viewers, and regularly use the technique of starting with the mystery and proceeding to unravel it.

If teachers start a lesson in this way, it means that the normal practice of sharing learning objectives with the students at the beginning is called into question. I have seen teachers using this technique who deliberately tell the students that the learning objectives will be 'discovered' during the lesson; indeed, in one of the best lessons of this type that I have observed, the students themselves defined the learning objectives in the plenary! This is a brilliant example of how the accepted wisdom on lesson starters should be treated as guidance rather than a set-in-concrete instruction.

## Starting with the finished product: how did we get there?

Another worthwhile approach to 'hook' the audience is to start with the finished product.

A teacher of Engineering or of Design and Technology might show an electronic robot as a starting point for a series of lessons on that subject, and a teacher of Drama might ask some older students to demonstrate some improvisation before developing those skills with others, but it is not only teachers of practical subjects that can do this:

- A teacher of English might read a gripping short story before introducing a class to the skills of creating writing.

- A teacher of Business Studies might look at a completed business plan before asking students to plan their own.

- A teacher of ICT might use a PowerPoint demonstration as an introduction to the skills of multimedia communication.

- A teacher of Basic Skills might look at a short description from a text before exploring the author's use of adjectives and adverbs.

- A teacher of Physical Education or Sports Science might ask an accomplished gymnast to demonstrate techniques on a trampoline at the beginning of a course for students new to the discipline.

- A teacher of Textiles or Design might introduce a 'brief' from an imaginary client to stimulate a range of possible designs.

# Sharing the aims of the lesson

## Oral explanation

All teachers will explain orally to the students what the task or activity is along with some prompts or examples. But not all students are good listeners and will they remember five minutes later?

## Whiteboard

Teachers will often accompany the oral explanation with some written aims on the whiteboard. The problem with this is that the aims may have to be rubbed off if the board is needed for other information. Some schools and colleges, to counter this problem, have invested in small whiteboards next to the main board where aims can be recorded and left throughout the lesson.

The only problem with this approach is that many teachers have a timetable with class after class arriving and leaving without respite during the day. As new classes arrive, instead of greeting students and supervising movement or seating arrangements, teachers are at the whiteboard, with their backs to students, trying to record the aims of the new lesson.

## Written handouts

Teachers may choose to copy the purpose of the task or activity onto a handout and give each student or pairs of students a copy. This is expensive however, both in terms of teacher time and copying costs.

## Poster or flipchart

An easier option is to use a piece of sugar paper or a sheet of flipchart paper. Use a thick felt-tip pen and record the aims on the poster/flipchart, which can be placed strategically in the room with sticky tack. These sheets can be recorded in advance of teaching and as one class leaves and another arrives, it is a simple matter to remove one sheet and replace it with the next.

(Thanks to Bernie Bramwell of Blurton High School for this simple but brilliant idea.)

Understand learning aims

## Express learning aims, not just the title or teacher objectives

Ensure that the purpose is expressed in terms of what students will learn, not in terms of teacher objectives or syllabus content. For example:

**Racism in our Society**

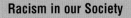 A title, not learning aims.

**By the end of this lesson you will:**

1. **Be more confident with key words.**

2. **Be able to explain how racism in our society can be seen in a variety of contexts.**

3. **Be able to explain some of the reasons why racism still exists.**

This flip chart has clear learning aims. Notice the first aim – key words. This can usefully be used for most lessons at all levels from infant to post-16.

If use of key words is included in the learning aims it will be clear why teachers are using activities such as:

Blockbusters (page 32)

Dominoes (page 54)

Whist (page 30)

Show Me Boards (page 40)

Matchmaker/Loop (page 36)

There are a number of ways in which lesson aims can be displayed in this way. The examples overleaf illustrate an approach to lesson aims that might be used in any subject or topic involving enquiry.

**Understand learning aims**

| 1800s: what were living conditions like? | *What?* |
|---|---|
| **What? How? Why?** | *Why?* |
| **Overcrowding** | |
| **Sanitation** | *When?* |
| **Disease** | *How do we know?* |
| **Laws** | |
| **Factories** | *Evidence?* |
| **Crime** | *Examples?* |
| **Children** | |
| **Working conditions** | *Causes?* |
| **Welfare** | *People?* |

In this example the lesson aims are expressed as a series of key words or issues. Alongside are some thinking tasks. Combine the two and a teacher might select a word such as 'disease' and invite students to use the words on the right to contribute ideas, examples or references they have found. Students quite enjoy this approach because it sets a real challenge for the lesson.

This approach also adds an air of mystery; 'we will be able to explain why these words are important by the end of the lesson…'

The benefit of this approach is that the teacher can point to the poster at regular intervals and introduce another word to be explored or discussed or can follow students' contributions by pointing to the words 'How do we know?' and inviting them to justify their ideas.

Understand learning aims

The approach can be used in a variety of contexts:

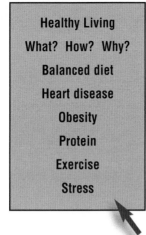

**Healthy Living**
What? How? Why?
**Balanced diet**
**Heart disease**
**Obesity**
**Protein**
**Exercise**
**Stress**

Such key words can be used as stimulus for class teaching, for questioning or research, and for any plenary that the teacher holds.

**Health and Safety**
What? How? Why?
**Electrical**
**Eyes**
**Machinery**
**Protection**
**Procedures**
**Rules**
**Records**

Such words can also be used by the teacher at the beginning of a lesson to stimulate discussion about prior learning and at the end to demonstrate progress. (The Snowball technique – see page 38 – would work well in conjunction with this lesson start idea.)

Understand learning aims

# Whist

Key words underpin learning and teaching in most topics at most levels and it is worth teachers investing time in building such vocabulary. Key words should be included in schemes of work, but once there should be revisited regularly if students are to become confident in their use. Card games are one approach and the example below uses Whist. Teachers and students will be able to think of others.

## Whist

This word game is best played in pairs and is based on the card game *Whist*. The teacher needs to prepare a set of playing cards that have on one side a key word or phrase. For example, the key word or phrase might be the name of a person, an object, a substance, a formula, a place, a piece of equipment, a word in a foreign language and many other things. On the card, below the word or phrase, is a question. The three examples below may help to illustrate this.

**1. Study of Macbeth**

## Duncan

The name of the King in Macbeth

**2. Study of volcanoes**

## Granite

The rock that is formed from slowly cooling magma

Key vocabulary

1   Multiple sets of cards should be prepared so that all students can play against a partner.

2   Each pair of students should be given ten different cards (the number can be higher or lower) and they should be shuffled. They are then dealt out so that each player has five cards.

3   Player One points to the back of one of Player Two's cards. Player Two reads out the question or definition. Player One tries to answer.

4   If the answer is correct then Player One wins the card and Player Two hands it over. Player One shuffles her cards so that the recently won card is mixed in with the others.

5   Player Two now points to one of Player One's cards and Player One asks a question. If Player Two answers correctly he wins that card and so the game progresses.

6   If a player answers incorrectly then the player asking the question keeps the card.

> **3. Vocabulary in a foreign language**
>
> # La Boulangerie
>
> Où on achète le pain?

This game of Whist is excellent, particularly for those with learning difficulties and/or poor self-esteem or low confidence. It is essentially a private game, with little stress but a fair degree of challenge. Both players develop the skills of speaking and listening.

**Key vocabulary**

# Blockbusters

The Blockbusters game, which is fondly remembered for Bob Holness and that famous quote "Can I have a 'P' please, Bob?" is brilliant for building the technical vocabulary of a subject discipline or vocational course. Students of all ages enjoy playing it and because they are engaged, they remember the definitions or technical terms – as in the answer oscillation, in the game below.

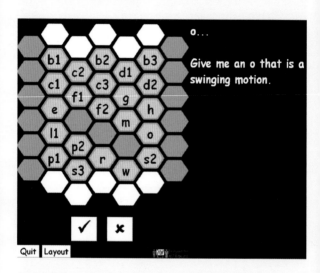

One of the remarkable features of this game is how many students remember the word a second time even if they didn't know it the first time the game was played. The game invariably motivates even the disaffected. The key point that needs to be made is that the *purpose* of the game is to build the literacy of the subject, not to keep students occupied. If the game were to be played as a time-filler, or simply as a distraction for an unruly class, it would serve little purpose. That is why the Blockbusters game, if used, needs to be integrated in the lesson planning so that the same words will appear at some time in the tasks, dialogue, activities, worksheets, text book or tests.

**Key vocabulary**

# Visual clues

Many students in a range of subjects will benefit from linking the key words with visuals. In the example below the word bevel is the answer to a visual clue in an engineering or mechanisms course.

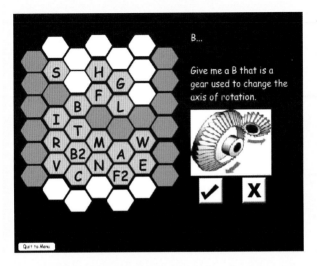

Teachers of modern languages or EFL know that learners often make connections between sounds, text and images. In the example below students can learn vocabulary in a topic on animals.

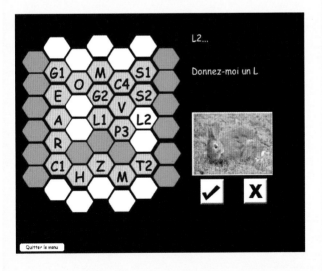

**Key vocabulary**

The game is stimulating and useful for the very young and for adults:

- Key words and images for Foundation or infants classes.
- Images and key words for a range of vocational subjects.

## Sound clues

The software also allows clues to be sounds – sound effects or voice. This allows teachers to record voice clues for weaker readers or use sound effects or WAV files in a range of subjects including Music. So all the clues can be spoken for non-readers or for students learning a foreign or additional language.

## Playing the game

In whole-class situations with the interactive version using interactive whiteboard or digital projector, it is best to organise two teams each with a captain. Explain that only the captain can give the answer, but that the teams can consult and so they might like to form a huddle. No one is to shout out.

The blue team connects across the screen and the orange team up and down. The letters are the first letter of the correct answer. If the team gets the answer right the teacher clicks on the tick at the bottom of the screen and the letter changes to the colour of that team. The same team has another go. If it gets the answer wrong the teacher clicks on the cross at the bottom of the screen and the letter changes to the other team's colour. That team now tries to answer that question. The game continues until one team connects across or down the screen when the whole screen flashes and the music plays.

The software comes with both the whole-class and individual games facility. If individuals choose to play against each other, they can select the 'individual' version where answers have to be typed in as in the example opposite.

The software allows teachers or students to create their own games but teachers who wish to save time can select from over 700 published games in 10 subjects for ages 7-16.

Key vocabulary

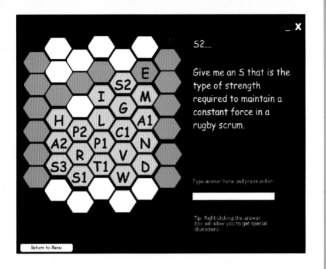

For more details on this software please go the resources section on page 144.

The Blockbusters games are based on the Thames Television programme Blockbusters. Licensed by Fremantle Brand Licensing www.fremantlemedia.com

Key vocabulary

# Matchmaker or the Loop

The 'loop' or 'matchmaker' activity is widely used in primary and secondary school numeracy lessons but can be adapted for any course to build the literacy of the subject.

## Matchmaker or Loop with words

In this Physical Education/Sports Science lesson, the teacher is rehearsing with the students the parts of the body that house key muscles.

Q: *Flex the knee*　　　A: *Hamstring*

Q: *Pectoral muscles*　　A: *Chest*

Q: *Biceps*　　　　　　A: *Arms*

Q: *Cardiac muscle*　　 A: *Heart*

The loop ends where it began.

| | |
|---|---|
| **Flex the knee** | **Heart** |
| **Pectoral muscles** | **Hamstring** |
| **Biceps** | **Chest** |
| **Cardiac muscle** | **Arms** |

Example:

*Student A:* 'flex the knee' *Student B:* 'hamstring'
*Student B:* 'pectoral muscles' *Student C:* 'chest'
and so on.

**Key vocabulary**

The activity works well at the beginning of a lesson, at the end or as a 'brain break' half way through a long double period. It works best if there is genuine pace – teachers may like to time the activity and try to beat the previous best. All students need to have a card and if anyone is absent then some students must have two – the loop will not complete if a card is on the teacher's desk.

The cards must be written carefully and the following system is best:

| | |
|---|---|
| The moon moves into the shadow of the Earth | 1 month |
| The name of our galaxy | Lunar Eclipse |
| Planet furthest from Sun | The Milky Way |
| Largest planet in solar system | Pluto |
| Phase of moon when moon is not visible | Jupiter |
| Most planets have these orbits | Gibbous |
| Earth's natural satellite | Elliptical |
| The length of Earth year in days | Moon |
| The number of planets in the solar system | 365 days |
| How long it takes for the moon to orbit the Earth | 9 planets |

The answer is one column below the question. Print out this table on card,, laminate and guillotine and the cards are ready to use.

Key vocabulary

# Snowball

The snowball is one of the simplest techniques teachers can use to encourage participation. Before looking at its various uses, it is worth explaining again how it works.

Stage 1: *On their own, students have to write down one example, idea or question asked for by the teacher. Students have 10 seconds.*

Stage 2: *Students move into pairs and work together to see if they can reach a total of 4 examples, ideas or questions. They have 30 seconds.*

Stage 3: *Students form a group of four and pooling their ideas, have to try and reach a total of 12 examples, ideas or questions. They have 60 seconds.*

When the process is complete the teacher will ask each group in turn to report one example, idea or question. This is better than asking one group to read out its list – this is demoralising for other groups who may have the same ideas.

The key purpose of a snowball is to encourage all students to participate: they should all be able to produce one idea (even if the teacher has to make a beeline for some students in the first 10 seconds and prompt them); they engage in dialogue in pairs and then in a small group.

## Brainstorming

The snowball can be used for brainstorming ideas – perhaps leading to the development of words or ideas for a mind map.

## Questions

Teachers regularly explain tasks to the class or ask students to read a handout or page from a textbook in silence. They then say 'any questions?' Few students will respond, even if they are unsure of something. The snowball is more effective.

*'Write down 1 question that you would like to ask for clarification.'*

*'In pairs, see if there is anything else you need help on...'*

*'In your group, combine all your questions and see if there are any more....'*

*'Now, group 1, ask me one question that would clarify something for your group...'*

In this way, through the safety of the group, students are more likely to ask for clarification than in the public arena of the classroom. Participation is higher.

## Review

It can also be used at the beginning of a lesson for re-capping on previous learning.

*'Write down 1 thing you learned last lesson about....'*

*'In pairs, see if the two of you can list a total of 4 things we learned last lesson about...'*

*'In your group, combine your lists and see if you can add 2 more things we learned about....'*

If you count the number of students involved at some stage in a snowball and compare it with the numbers involved in a traditional hands-up approach, there is no contest; the snowball wins hands down.

# Give us a Clue and True or False

One of the challenges faced by many teachers is to encourage students to read closely. The short-response test regime that dominates certain areas and phases in education requires students to scan documents in order to find 'the answer', and as a result many young people find it difficult to read closely for understanding.

The 'Give us a clue' activity is simple to operate and does encourage close study of text or documents. The teacher asks the students, probably in pairs in a big class, to study the document and find a piece of information that they understand. They are then asked to write three clues to what this information is in order for others in the class to study the document and find the information.

## Example: Geography – Ordinance Survey maps

In pairs, students study an Ordinance Survey map and find a location of their own choice. One pair chooses a location and sets the following clues:

1  This village has two churches, one with a spire.

2  This same village also has a very steep hill to the North West.

3  This village has a railway line to the south east.

*What is the village?*
In order to find the village the other groups will have to study the map closely and use their understanding of symbols to find a village that fits the clues.

The same process can be used in a range of subjects and with all levels. For example:

- The name of a chemical or process in Science.
- The name of a famous economist, philosopher, mathematician, sociologist, politician, scientist, psychologist, artist, musician, sportsman or sportswoman.
- A treaty or event in History.

- A piece of equipment in engineering or other vocational area.
- The name of a character in a novel or play.
- A person in the class in modern foreign languages.

Teachers will find many other uses for this activity that requires students to participate, to study documents for their own clues, and to study the same documents to solve clues presented by others.

## True or false?

A variation of this activity is True or False? The same process is followed with students studying a document, map, diagram or photograph and then working out a statement based on their study. Other groups are asked to decide if the statement is true or false based on their own understanding.

This can produce wonderful debate because, as you will soon come to realise if you try it out, some information can be interpreted differently and it can lead to lively discussion as groups try to defend or attack statements that are made.

One thing is for sure; all individuals participate and they will not quickly forget what they have learned.

The True or False activity can be combined with Show Me Boards, widely used in schools. When one pair or group reads out its statement, the other students respond with their Show Me Boards.

# Question Time

Question Time is a variant on *Hot Seating*, well known in Drama. In Question Time, however, questions are addressed to a group or panel, not to an individual.

This activity is excellent for participation in questioning sessions when the teacher wants to review learning at the end of a lesson, a topic or even a whole term or year. It also shows how teachers who ask all the questions are missing the learning opportunities that clearly emerge when students take on this role.

Students are asked to form pairs or small teams of three or four. Ideally these teams will be structured carefully so that they are mixed in terms of skills or confidence. One group is selected to be the 'experts' (or as in the BBC programme Question Time, the 'panel'), and are told that in, for example, fifteen minutes time the other groups will ask them questions on the topic/area prescribed by the teacher. The Question Time 'experts' now begin revising the topic, trying to anticipate questions and working out what answers they will give.

The other groups are told to prepare questions for the 'experts' and are told they must themselves work out the answers before they are allowed to put any questions to other groups. They collaborate on formulating questions and agree the order in which they will speak when the plenary takes place.

Both the groups asking the questions and the group responding as the 'panel' gain much from this activity. *Asking* questions is as much about learning as *answering* questions, and teachers who try this with a class will be amazed how intense the debate and discussion becomes. The groups asking the questions will be determined to '*go for the jugular*' – to ask the hardest possible questions they can – while the students on the 'panel' will be trying their very best not to get caught out.

When the questions are asked, the panel's response should always first be referred to the group that asked the question to see if they are happy with the answer given. In that way the teacher plays the part of 'Chairperson' and 'Mediator', ruling when there are disputes, but not dominating the proceedings.

The teacher can decide to change the 'panel' at any time with phrases like: "That was a brilliant question. I think your group ought to become the 'experts' now." Question Time will work in any subject and for any level. For example:

- Bank managers answering questions on setting up a small business.
- Building inspectors or health and safety experts answering questions from clients.
- Healthy-eating consultants at a health clinic.
- Historians taking questions from amateur historians.
- Town planners taking questions from the public.
- Town guides taking questions beginning 'Où est…' in a modern languages lesson.
- Statisticians taking questions on a set of data.
- Music or Art experts on some aspect of their subject.
- Experts in a particular faith or culture.

*Peer assessment*
The Question Time activity can also be used to develop peer assessment (see page 128). It is particularly useful when small groups have collaborated on a project or presentation. Other groups can focus their questions on issues such as:

- How well the project meets the set criteria.
- How and why decisions were made.

*And so on…*

# Pass the Question

This is a superb activity that in my experience never fails to stimulate students at any age or level. It works well as a plenary to a lesson or as a revision exercise for an individual topic or for the whole course, depending upon the circumstances. In large classes it is best conducted in pairs but for smaller classes the students can work individually.

The teacher asks the students (e.g. in pairs) to revise the topic under consideration and then to think up a question on the topic that will have to be answered by another pair in the class. They are also required to work out answers to their own questions.

The teacher needs to prepare **two** sets of playing cards numbered 1-15. (The reason for 2 sets will become clear.)

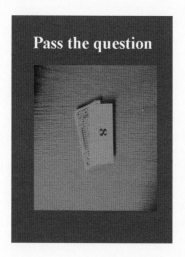

**Pass the question**

The best way to produce the cards is to buy printer labels nearly the same size as playing cards and use the labels facility in Office to print out labels that you stick on existing cards and then trim to size.

All the pairs are then allocated a number (e.g. in a class of 30 students, all pairs will have a number somewhere between 1 and 15). The teacher then shuffles the cards and turns one over to reveal the number (e.g. 8). The teacher asks:

*"What is your question, pair 8?"*

**Participation**

**44**

Pair 8 asks their question. The teacher can, at this point, heighten the tension by saying something like:

> *"What a good question. Really hard! Who, I wonder, is going to have to answer that one?"*

All the other pairs are currently thinking about the question because until the next card is turned over, no one knows who has to respond. The teacher eventually turns over the next card and reveals the number (e.g. 12). The teacher continues to engage the class:

> *"Right, pair 12, what is your answer?"*

Pair 12 answers and the teacher asks pair 8 to tell the class whether it is right or not. There may be debate at any point, which will be chaired by the teacher. Then the teacher asks pair 12 to ask their question and the teacher turns over the next card. And in this way all students will be required to ask a question and to answer one… except pair 8 who had the first card to be revealed. That is why teachers need two packs of numbered cards. When number 8 is turned over the teacher quickly holds up Pack Two and takes the 8 out, placing it somewhere in the middle of Pack One. In that way pair 8 will also be asked a question later.

In order to maintain the concentration of those who answer a question early on, the teacher may also take three or four more cards out of Pack Two, not revealing which, of course, and shuffle them into Pack One. In this way all students know that at least four numbers are in twice and will continue to listen and think in case their number reappears.

The level of concentration in this activity is quite remarkable. If teachers compare it with the normal situation with the teacher asking all the questions:

> *"David, tell me what…."*

David is now listening intently, but no one else is. Why should they? In the mind of each student is the thought 'it is David's problem, not mine!'

## Pass the question – alternative approaches

One of the potential problems with the pass the question activity described previously is that in a mixed-ability class, it would be possible for a really challenging question devised by two confident students to be presented to a pair of students lacking in skills or confidence and this could be quite damaging to their self-esteem. Pass the question for such students might be a source of considerable anxiety and so flexibility is needed if teachers want to make use of it.

One option is to organise the pairs so that more confident students work in partnership with students who have less confidence. This might, however, limit the degree of challenge that more able students might wish to put into their questions. Another alternative is to run the same exercise without the playing cards and use paper instead.

Students are given an A4 sheet and asked to fold it down the middle. On the top half of the sheet they are required to put their names and then devise their questions or problems. At the bottom they need to record their answers. When they are ready they ask the teacher to check what they have created, and if the teacher is happy she/he rips off the top half of the sheet with the question on and allocates it to another pair of students who have to work out the answers.

---

1 Why should you not use chipped or cracked equipment for food?
2 What should the temperature of a fridge be?
3 At which temperature do bacteria grow?
4 How often can you reheat cooked food?
5 What happens to bacteria below 5°C?

---

### Answers

1 Because bacteria can hide in the cracks and chips.
2 Between 2°C and 5°C.
3 10°C to 65°C.
4 Only once.
5 They do not multiply but are not destroyed.

The benefit of this approach for classes of widely differing levels of confidence or skills is that the teacher allocates the questions to students based on her/his knowledge of (a) the degree of difficulty of the questions and (b) the confidence levels of the individuals or pairs. All students are involved in asking and answering questions and in this example little stress is experienced by those with low confidence because (a) the exercise is not public and (b) the questions are more likely to be within their capability.

# Activexpression

## Electronic participation

Response handsets are often called 'voting pads' for the obvious reason that early generations of the technology such as Activote and Quizdom simply allowed users to vote for an answer (e.g. multiple choice) or to register an opinion (e.g. agree/disagree).

Activexpression continues to offer the voting function, but multiple choice is now much more sophisticated, offering users a range of new options. It can be used with up to 500 handsets at once with just a digital projector, computer and screen. Results and analysis are displayed on the computer screen or whiteboard.

But the developments that will have the biggest impact upon engagement and participation are *texting* and *self-paced learning*, leading to Real Time Personalised Instruction (RTPI).

The texting and numeric keyboard is a revelation. Most young people are used to texting and they really enjoy participating with Activexpression.

RTPI, unique to Promethean's Activexpression, is examined in the Outstanding Learning section under *differentiation through ICT*, on page 96, but the texting function will be examined here.

The keyboard permits learners to use 'text' mode to key in and send ideas, feelings, questions or answers. This means that for those fortunate enough to have access to the technology, the hands-up approach where only four or five learners willingly participate is turned into an activity where ideas from everyone appear on the screen.

Outstanding Teaching

48

"What kinds of food are bad for you if you eat a lot of them?" asks the teacher.

All learners text their ideas and the analysis shows who sent which idea.

Activexpression has 5 language options including French, German and Spanish. In a Cloze exercise in French, the teacher asks learners to suggest a word for the gap.

"Je vais…… au parc avec mes amis." All participate by texting a suggestion.

Activexpression also has a numeric function. In mental maths –

"What is 6 squared?" - all participate using the keyboard.

The rank in order (importance, chronology) function will be well used.

"Rank these 5 causes of population increase in order of importance 1 to 5."

In all cases the software produces an instant analysis of all responses that can be tabulated and pasted to the screen. It also provides teacher with a 'who sent what response' table. This superb technology provides the answer to those teachers who seek 100% participation in a class and the full analysis of each and every contribution helps them to provide instant 'live' feedback to learners.

For a free demonstration of Activexpression in your school, please email info@robertpowellpublications.com ref Activexpression.

Participation

# Support groups

(The purpose and composition of Support groups are explained in detail on page 68.)

Earlier it was made clear that shared learning aims were a key principle for the beginning of lessons. In the example below the learning aims were displayed on the classroom wall and explained at the beginning of the lesson. It is critical that the teacher revisits them during or at the end of the lesson to assess and celebrate the progress made by individual students.

> By the end of this lesson you will be able to answer the questions:
>
> 1 What were conditions like for the poor in London's slums in the 1800s?
> 2 How did the Industrial Revolution contribute to these conditions?
> 3 What were the key words?

Traditionally teachers may review learning with a short question/answer session with contributions from the regular 'volunteers' or a few of the 'conscripts' selected by the teacher. Participation is not high and it is difficult for the teacher to judge what progress in learning most students have made.

The use of **support groups** can improve participation in this process of review. The teacher, pointing to the lesson aims on the wall, says to the class:

*"We said at the beginning of the lesson that by the end of this session we would be able to describe the living conditions for the poor in slums in London in the 1800s. In your support groups please list as many examples as you can. You have 3 minutes. Off you go."*

**Review learning**

If students are seated in rows then students turn their chairs around to face the others in their support group. The Chairperson now asks the question *"What living conditions do we know about?"* The Scribe now records ideas, putting in brackets next to the idea the initials of the person who suggested it. (This process is described in Teaching on page 16.)

| Living Conditions | |
|---|---|
| poor or no sanitation | Karla |
| Disease from rats | Asif |

This activity is safe - individuals contribute within the confines of the group and the teacher, who will usually be patrolling the classroom prompting and cajoling, can see who has contributed to the review of learning. When the three minutes are up the teacher calls a plenary and asks each table in turn to contribute one example of living conditions until all the ideas are exhausted. This 'plenary' will have involved all students and will clearly demonstrate the learning that has taken place. If the ideas are recorded on a flip-chart sheet, an interactive whiteboard or OHP then the teacher can return to them next lesson.

If the teacher chooses, each individual in the group can be asked to contribute to the feedback. Learning can be enhanced if individuals report back on the ideas of others in the group. This will encourage peer coaching and deeper understanding.

# Reveal

This is a group activity that works well with support groups or pairs in the case of a small class. (See pages 50 and 68 for more on Support Groups.) The teacher has prepared in advance a list of 10 key points from the previous lesson and printed them on acetate. This is placed on an OHP covered by a piece of card.

## Ten things we know about the skeletal system

1.  The skeleton has four functions: support, protection, movement and blood production.
2.  There are four types of bone: long, short, flat and irregular.
3.  There are three different types of joints: fixed or immovable, slightly movable, freely movable.

The teacher asks each group at the end of the lesson to spend three minutes together trying to list the ten things they think they have learnt about the skeletal system.

When the time is up, the teacher reveals her/his list one at a time by sliding the card down on the overhead projector. The task for the students is to match the teacher's list. When this activity is used it invariably leads to groups celebrating when they match the points listed by the teacher. Some groups are also keen to list points that the teacher has forgotten or omitted. It is an excellent activity both for a progress review and for participation.

The template is very easy to produce and the activity does not take long once the students know the system. It can also be used as a lesson starter where the teacher asks students to list ten points from the previous lesson as in the following example using an interactive whiteboard.

# Interactive whiteboards

The Reveal activity described in this section can be used on the Promethean ACTIVboard by utilising the 'blind' facility that the Promethean software provides. The text or images are hidden behind what is best described as a living room blind. In the same way as you can draw a blind to reveal the sunlight, so you can use the pen (a computer mouse in the shape of a pen) to bring down the blind as slowly or as quickly as you choose to reveal the text or images behind. The example below is from a Geography unit on earthquakes where the students have to identify 10 things they have learnt about the characteristics of plates.

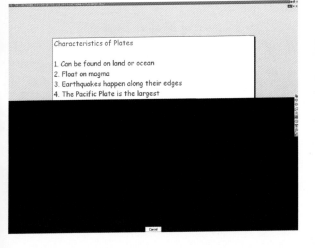

# Dominoes

The Dominoes game can be used at any point in a lesson for consolidating learning, for initiating discussion or for revision. It can also be used at the end of a lesson or unit of work as a means of reviewing the learning progress that has been made.

In the Dominoes game the teacher places a combination of 20 words or images onto 10 dominoes as in the example below on the topic 'Healthy Eating', where images rather than words have been used.

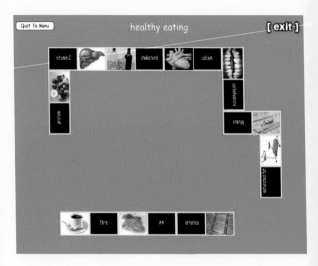

The activity can be organised in many ways, but below is a suggestion that works well if playing the game with an interactive whiteboard or with digital projector and screen.

1   Small groups of three or four students are organised by the teacher and allocated a number – Group 1, Group 2, etc.

2   The 10 dominoes with 20 words and/or images are displayed at the bottom of the screen.

3   The teacher drags out one domino (e.g. image of alcohol next to the word cholesterol) to the top of the screen and invites Group 1 to suggest a word or image from one of the dominoes at the

**Review learning**

bottom that has a link with one of the words or images at the top.

4   Group 1 suggests a word or image (e.g. image of liver next to image of alcohol) and the teacher asks someone from the group to justify the link.

5   If the explanation is accepted the teacher praises the group and one of the students from that group comes out and moves the domino adjacent to the one suggested. One point is awarded to Group 1.

6   Group 2 is now invited to make a link and so on.

Both card and software versions of the Dominoes game stimulate students and a range of skills is developed:

1   An understanding of key words or images.

2   An understanding of how individual words or images relate to other words or images within a unit.

3   Students are required to work collaboratively, discussing and debating possible links.

4   It develops an ability to explain those links to others, to defend an argument on occasions, and to challenge others to do the same.

5   Because the game requires students to move cards on a table or dominoes on a screen, it is supporting those who enjoy kinaesthetic activity.

Details of the published dominoes games and the software to create your own is included in the resources section on page 144.

# Student-led Review

One of the approaches that teachers might adopt is to ask a small group of students to lead a plenary using the original aims of the lesson as the agenda for a review of the learning. This can be handled in a number of ways but one example is offered.

1 A small group of students volunteer to lead the plenary and begin by reminding the class of the lesson aims by pointing to them on the flipchart.

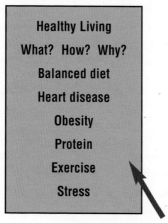

**Healthy Living**
**What? How? Why?**
**Balanced diet**
**Heart disease**
**Obesity**
**Protein**
**Exercise**
**Stress**

They might begin by asking the class to brainstorm key words in relation to *healthy living*, which they record on the whiteboard.

2 The Chair of the group then begins the plenary by selecting one of the words and saying something like:

*"We did some research on this and found that..."*

and outlines some of the issues identified by her/his group.

*"Would someone from another group like to select another word and tell us something else they found...?"*

3 They involve other groups at all times by asking for further details or examples which help to illustrate any point.

4　If an interactive whiteboard is in use the students leading the plenary can add the words and the details or examples to a flipchart (with the text recognition tool if available) so that the words and examples are saved.

5　The notes prepared by the group on the whiteboard can then be printed out for everyone.

This type of plenary encourages participation and is led and dominated by students, not by the teacher.

## Other activities

Many of the interactive strategies described elsewhere in the handbook can be used in a review of learning at the end of a lesson:

- Blockbusters (page 32 to review understanding of key words).
- Question time (page 42 a shortened version with just one question from each group).
- Snowball (page 38 for collating key points of learning).
- Show me boards (page 40 for key words, formulae, mental mathematics, spelling).
- Visual map (page 20 asking students to talk the class through the journey).

# Assessment Review

The plenary or 'what have we learned today?' review will be a useful exercise for teachers who have set a clearly identified set of learning aims and want to assess individuals' learning and how successful the lesson has been.

## Review of independent or small group work

There are numerous occasions, however, when students have been working on an independent or small group basis, planning, developing, making or designing, where it is much more difficult for the teacher to review progress on a whole-class basis.

On these occasions a plenary that focuses on a review of learning aims may not be appropriate because each student or group may have an entirely different set of aims.

This does not mean, however, that a plenary might not be useful. If the focus was not on individual aims but on assessment issues, a plenary might serve a very useful purpose.

For example, students designing or making a product in a practical subject may be working towards different products, but all will be governed by the same course or examination criteria. A teacher might usefully pose a number of questions to all individuals or groups on issues related to assessment:

- *Can anyone give me an example of how you are meeting the criteria for your project?*

- *What have you done that you think will enable you to meet the criteria for a higher grade or level?*

- *Which criteria are you finding it difficult to interpret?*

- *How in practice have you improved your project from the original design or plan?*

Such questions may only take a few minutes but they provide a useful and unifying theme for all students to reflect upon their progress.

## Problem forum

Many students working on individual projects may struggle on occasions to maintain their momentum, to tackle complex issues or to work their way through relatively tedious sections of their overall work. "The loneliness of the independent learner" springs to mind. Plenaries, or indeed reviews half way through a long session, can sometimes re-energise proceedings.

Teachers might usefully hold a regular 'problem forum' when students are invited to ask for advice or help from others in solving a problem that they are facing with their project. These questions can be posed orally in an open forum or, if students or teachers prefer, in writing to the teacher.

---

**Please help...**

*I need help on rotating text - Jo*

*I need help on re-sizing images - Bhuna*

*I don't know how to use video editor - Chin*

---

Teachers can also use a small notice board as a **Please help...** facility during independent work. Students sign up with a problem and someone who can help offers to do so. Once solved, the problem is erased from the board.

# Celebration Review

I can think of no better way to build self-esteem, to develop confidence, to cultivate a sense of pride in work, to improve motivation and to strengthen relationships than to hold a plenary that seeks to celebrate progress, success or creativity.

Such a celebration can take many forms:

- Asking students to show others what they have designed or made.
- Allowing students to explain their innovative approach to a problem.
- Rewarding with public praise the progress of students who have persevered despite finding the task a real challenge.

Many colleagues will recognise the potential flaws with such agendas:

- Young men or boys embarrassed with public praise
- Abuse for the 'swot'
- The isolation of those whose work is never praised
- The potential for ridicule.

That is not a reason to desist from such agendas, but teachers must handle them with care and great sensitivity. They will be helped in this if such proceedings begin at junior school, continue throughout secondary education and extend into post-16 and adult education. No one should ever be allowed to feel embarrassed about making good progress.

## Whole-class celebrations

One of the ways to celebrate whole-class achievement is through the use of the student response system described in more detail on page 70.

A quick test at the beginning of the lesson using the handsets pictured can identify individuals' prior knowledge or learning. The software produces data that can be exported directly into Excel.

Review learning

### Before the teaching

| User | Total | % | Total Response Time | Q1 (C) | Q2 (C) | Q3 (A) | Q4 (D) |
|------|-------|----|--------------------|--------|--------|--------|--------|
| Don | 2 | 50 | 00:00:39 | A | D | A | D |
| Cloe | 3 | 75 | 00:00:39 | C | B | A | D |
| Michelle | 2 | 50 | 00:00:38 | B | C | A | B |
| Ann-Marie | 1 | 25 | 00:00:37 | C | A | C | C |
| Curtis | 2 | 50 | 00:00:40 | D | B | D | D |
| Amir | 1 | 25 | 00:00:37 | D | B | A | C |
| Naomi | 0 | 0 | 00:00:37 | A | D | B | B |
| Barry | 1 | 25 | 00:00:37 | B | D | A | A |

| User | Total | % | Total Response Time | Q1 (C) | Q2 (C) | Q3 (A) | Q4 (D) |
|------|-------|----|--------------------|--------|--------|--------|--------|
| Don | 3 | 75 | 00:00:43 | C | D | A | D |
| Cloe | 4 | 100 | 00:00:39 | C | C | A | D |
| Michelle | 3 | 75 | 00:00:36 | C | D | A | D |
| Ann-Marie | 2 | 50 | 00:00:42 | C | A | A | C |
| Curtis | 3 | 75 | 00:00:50 | D | C | A | D |
| Amir | 2 | 50 | 00:00:46 | C | B | A | C |
| Naomi | 2 | 50 | 00:00:55 | A | C | A | B |
| Barry | 3 | 75 | 00:00:51 | C | D | A | D |

**After the teaching (More details on the handsets in the Resources section page 144.)**

The use of such immediate feedback on success is excellent both for teachers and for students who can leave the lesson cheered by the knowledge that progress has been made.

There will be those, of course, who do not make progress but this is an opportunity for a number of interventions on the part of teachers or learning assistants.

- After school revision clubs.
- Small group tutorials in the next lesson (see section on oral feedback on page 138).
- Modified tasks in the following lessons.

Although a lack of progress can be demoralising for students, the knowledge that the teacher is aware and offering support will reduce the anxiety. Sometimes the lack of understanding is not communicated and the teaching moves on regardless, a cause of some considerable stress to learners.

# Learning logs

In example 1, these primary school pupils have just completed a series of science lessons on living and growing. They then summarise their learning in a visual learning log. One is reproduced here.

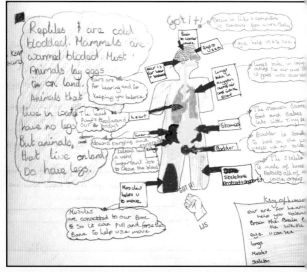

Thanks are due to pupils and staff at Inglehurst Junior School in Leicester for the use of this example. More information on their website www.learninglogs.co.uk.

> When I get home I open my learning log straight away because it is so much fun. Sometimes I am so absorbed in my work I do it at the table with my dinner.

> I like learning logs because they remind you about what you have learnt. I have been working on The Hound of the Baskervilles. I have put string in my learning log to show that the hound is chasing Sir Henry.

**Review learning**

I really enjoy using colour, pop-ups and touchy/feely things to make my learning log more personal and unique.

This log will serve both to deepen understanding and also to act as a revision tool for tests. The feedback provided in the log also allows the teacher to assess the child's learning, a much quicker appraisal than is often the case.

Parents also get involved in reading the learning logs and working with their children when developing a log for homework. There is no doubt that the approach is sold on the children. The quotes dotted around the page from children at Inglehurst Junior School sum up in the best possible way how learning logs can contribute to learning and motivation.

"When our teachers mark them they know what we need help with."

"You can personalise your log so you understand it. I think learning logs are great because you can develop your own style, which makes yours different to everybody else's. They are great for SATs revision."

"I think learning logs are a great way of storing good and important ideas. I spend at least an hour a day on my learning log. I complete all my objectives and then decorate it. They are great fun to work with and are very personal."

I enjoy doing my learning log because we can talk to our teachers through our learning log.

Review learning

# *Outstanding...*

| Principle | The Challenge |
|---|---|
| **1.** Ensure that all individual students are clear when tasks or activities begin. | Learners will be unable to make progress and personal confidence will be damaged if they are unclear on any aspect of the learning activities planned by the teacher. |
| **2.** Ensure that tasks designed to develop understanding involve thinking and processing. | Effective learning takes place only when students make sense of or process new learning or skills. If the purpose of a task is to develop understanding, it must do more than simply demand answers; tasks to develop understanding will often be different from those that are used to test understanding. |
| **3.** Meet the needs of individuals through effective differentiation. | There are often huge variations in the levels of skill and confidence in the classroom. Teachers should ensure that the planning of tasks includes provision for those who might need further support or additional challenge. |
| **4.** Integrate basic and key skills when possible. | Skills developed in real contexts tend to be assimilated more successfully, and all teachers should aim to build basic and key skills through their normal teaching programme. |

# Learning

# Traffic lights and Emperor techniques

For effective learning to take place, teachers must share clear learning aims with the students, and examples of how to do this are presented in the section on Teaching on page 126.

When students begin to work on a task or an activity set by the teacher, however, they must be absolutely clear about what it is the teacher wants them to do. The 'Are you clear?' question from the teacher is not guaranteed to elicit a truthful response. There are a number of approaches that can be used.

## Traffic lights

This technique is used quite successfully, usually with younger students. All students are issued with three cards, one red, one amber, and one green. At any point in the lesson the teacher can ask students to express their degree of understanding by asking them to hold up one of the cards: red means little understanding, amber means fair understanding, and green means full understanding.

**Green.**
**I am OK. I understand.**

**Amber.**
**I understand some of it.**

**Red.**
**I don't understand at all.**

Ensure clarity

## Emperor approach

Some teachers use a variation on the cards by asking students to indicate clarity with their thumbs. Like the Emperor in ancient Rome, thumbs up for understanding, thumbs sideways for some understanding and thumbs down for little understanding.

Teachers of older students will find that the use of support groups (page 68) and the electronic feedback facility (page 70) are more appropriate for judging the degree of clarity.

Thumbs up.
I understand.

Thumbs sideways.
I understand some of it.

Thumbs down.
I don't understand at all.

Ensure clarity

# Support groups

The Support Groups approach to this problem is a more sophisticated approach than the Traffic Lights/Emperor techniques and will work for most subjects and for any age group. The process works as follows:

1. The class must be organised into small groups of about four students, with each group containing someone who is relatively confident and someone who might need support.

2. In selecting effective groups, teachers will obviously need to take into account relationships, cultural issues, behaviour issues and so on. The main criterion is that the chosen groups will work.

3. You do not need group tables for this technique to work. If the classroom has tables set out in rows, all teachers need to do is organise the seating so that one pair sits behind or in front of the other pair in their support group.

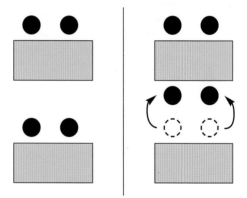

4. Each support group should have someone who takes on the role of Chairperson, and someone who is the Scribe – it is best to rotate these roles if possible. (For more on this see pages 14 and 16.)

5. The teacher now says: "Before we start the task, join your support group and check that we are all clear about what we have to do."

6   The Chairperson now asks the question, "Are we all clear?" In the safety of the group, individuals can now express any concerns and these are noted by the Scribe. If members of the group are able to help others, they do so. If, however, all members of the group are confused, the Chairperson asks the teacher for support.

The key point is that this process is safe:

- Individuals are more likely to be honest and ask for clarification with people they trust.
- The request for help comes from the Chairperson.
- The group gets clarification together – good use of time.
- Peer support is encouraged – reducing anxiety.

This process is not perfect but it does make a difference and contributes greatly to making the classroom a 'safer' environment.

## Snowball

This technique is described in more detail on page 38. The snowball can be use to encourage questions for clarity, maybe as a follow-up to electronic feedback (see page 70).

1   Individuals are given 15 seconds (negotiable) to think of one question that would help them have better understanding. Throughout the snowball process the teacher circulates, prompting those who might benefit from support.

2   Once the time is up, students are told to work in pairs for 30 seconds (pace is critical) and try and find two more questions that they would like answering, trying to get to a total of four.

3   Once the time is up the pairs join the other pair in their support group and all groups are now given two minutes to try and reach a total of 10 questions.

4   The teacher holds a report-back session, taking one question from each group in turn.

Ensure clarity

# Electronic feedback

The student response system that allows students to respond in a variety of situations using an electronic handset is also examined on page 116. The technology, however, is wonderful for encouraging learners to respond truthfully and in total anonymity to the question *"..are you clear?"*

The Promethean handsets have a voting pad A-F. So students can vote in the range from 'A' (I am totally clear) to 'F' (I am totally confused) giving feedback on the range of confidence in the classroom.

## Anonymity

When teachers use this electronic system they have an option for 'named' or 'anonymous' reports, and so the question can be answered truthfully without any anxiety. The bar chart that the system displays immediately after the voting has taken place will provide instant and informative feedback, allowing teachers to proceed or revisit depending upon the responses.

## Are you clear ?

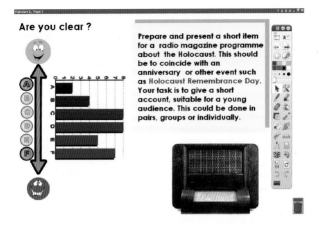

Prepare and present a short item for a radio magazine programme about the Holocaust. This should be to coincide with an anniversary or other event such as Holocaust Remembrance Day. Your task is to give a short account, suitable for a young audience. This could be done in pairs, groups or individually.

The 'are you clear?' question has produced feedback that says quite clearly 'not yet!' The teacher can now use a technique like the snowball (see page 38) to identify in an equally safe manner what the concerns are.

The handsets can also be used to evaluate individuals' views on their strengths and weaknesses. Here, 'C and D' are obviously perceived problems for many learners.

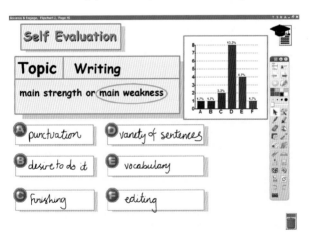

Although the responses are anonymous, the teacher is still able to identify the individual responses, and this can lead to support being targeted.

Ensure clarity

# Tasks to develop understanding

## Tasks to test or to develop understanding?

Many of the strategies set out in this section on thinking and processing need to be set into the context that many teachers face in their daily challenges in classrooms. One of these challenges concerns the distinction between tasks designed to *test* understanding and tasks designed to *develop* understanding.

## Tasks to test understanding

One of the major responsibilities for teachers and support staff at all levels is to prepare learners for tests and examinations. The degree of testing in education has grown significantly and the questions in many of the tests require only a short response from students. There are, in my view, two main reasons for this growth in the short response test:

1   Such a format allows examiners to ask questions on a wide range of topics thus ensuring 'coverage' of the syllabus.

2   Such tests are easier and cheaper to mark. Once you move away from the right/wrong answers into professional judgements, all kinds of problems emerge with accuracy, consistency and cost.

So, if tests and examinations are dominated by short response questions, it is entirely reasonable that teachers prepare students for this with regular use of worksheets that demand such responses. It is also quite understandable why so many publishers of text books include so many low-level, short response questions in the 'things to do' sections. The examples below will be familiar to most teachers:

Fill in the missing word…               (1 mark for each)
Complete this sentence….               (2 marks)
Give me 3 reasons why…               (3 marks)
Look at the diagram. Tick the 2 boxes below which have true statements.               (2 marks)

## Tasks to develop understanding

There is every justification for such worksheets and 'things to do' tasks if these are the types of questions students will face in tests and examinations. But there is a problem that teachers should identify and guard against:

1   Such tasks are designed to test understanding, but they will do little to help develop understanding.

2   If worksheets/tasks such as these dominate the daily experience of learners then we should not be surprised that so many find extended writing a challenge. Essays, investigations, projects and evaluations – all these activities demand thinking, analysing and processing, and such skills must be developed with regular practice and support.

Teachers must ensure a 'mixed economy', where a balance is maintained between preparing for tests with practice in low-level tasks, and developing real learning and deeper understanding with tasks designed to make students think. In planning tasks teachers must ask themselves a key question:

Is the purpose of this task to **test** understanding or to **develop** it?

Other examples in this section look at the latter; tasks that involve processing and thinking, leading to deeper understanding and an ability to cope more easily with extended writing assignments.

# Processing handouts

Many studies show that effective learning requires students to connect new knowledge or skills with existing knowledge; thinking and processing are central to this.

The challenge for teachers, however, is that many worksheets and 'things to do' sections in published textbooks and resources are often dominated by low-level questions and tasks that require little thought or processing.

## Processing handouts

Handouts are commonly used in all phases of education, but most often post-16. Handouts vary enormously in quality but unless the students process the contents, there is a danger that they leave the lesson with a fat folder but little understanding. One approach that ensures that this doesn't happen is to think carefully about the layout of the handout.

Characteristics:

- Long lines, closely typed text – too long for the eye to cope with.
- Students scan rather than read for understanding.
- No headings or breaks to make the text less daunting.
- No illustrations or white space to help it appeal to the eye.

Thinking and processing

- No space for learners to add their own information.

One of the main problems with poor handouts is that the work has been done by the teacher. The processes that lead to learning and deeper understanding – the thinking, the analysis, the selection and prioritising of information – all have been done by the teacher and not by the students. Unless a way can be found to ensure that learners process the contents and develop the deeper insights that lead to longer-term understanding then the time and effort it took to create may have been wasted.

The handout below has been reorganised to ensure that processing takes place.

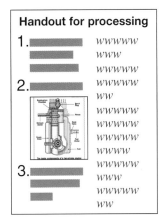

Characteristics:
- The information has been separated into sections.
- Space separates the paragraphs.
- An illustration has been added.
- Only half the handout has been used for the information (left-hand side).
- The right has been left blank.
- During the lesson the teacher asks students to discuss each section, clarifying, questioning, citing examples, etc.
- Students add their own notes in the space on the right.
- They are processing the handout, making it their own, not the teacher's.

Thinking and processing

# Reworking notes

*"A lecture is a process whereby the information moves from the lecturer's notes to the student's notes without passing through the brain of either."*

This practice still takes place – often for very good reasons. Indeed, a powerful lecture or presentation can engage students and do much to stimulate the desire for learning and further exploration.

Not all notes, however, lead to deeper understanding. One way teachers can ensure that the same notes are processed and made sense of is to insist that once students have completed the notes they should be asked to rework them into a different format.

One example, taken from a brilliant textbook *Modern World History, The Teacher's Resource Book* (First Edition) by Ben Walsh, is worth presenting here.

The topic is the First World War, and students are required to do some personal reading and research on the state of Germany in 1918. Students must examine a range of problems facing Germany, including the emergence of the fascists, the pressure from the communists, the economic problems, problems with the infrastructure, and relationships with neighbouring countries.

Students have access to textbooks, related literature and maybe the Internet. They will also have taken notes during some of the lessons on this issue. But what they have to do with the information they collect is to produce their own version of a pie chart supplied by the teacher:

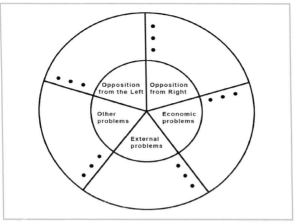

Thanks to John Murray Publishers

- All the segments are currently of equal size.
- Students have to resize the slices of the pie to reflect the reality.
- They have to place three points of evidence on the outer rim bullet points.
- They have to produce an image (ICT or OHP transparency) of their finished product.
- Other groups will have done versions and each group must present and justify its conclusions and evidence.

The important point about this activity is that students are required to make or take notes, to process them, to evaluate the evidence and then to present and justify their conclusions.

This is not the only type of processing that can be used with notes or handouts. All the products below will require students to display deeper understanding:

- A grid or a matrix.
- A hierarchy e.g. most important to least important.
- A 'for' and 'against' table with evidence or justification.
- A summary of key points.
- A speech or presentation.
- A visual map (more on this on page 20).

Thinking and processing

# Tension graphs

Teachers of English Literature may be familiar with this activity. Students are required to represent the tension in a play or novel by producing a line graph that plots the events. For example, the graph opposite has been produced by a student as a result of reading and discussion of *An Inspector Calls*.

The teacher had issued a set of cards describing events in the play. These were shuffled and students were first required to place them in chronological order and then number them, shown in the table below. Students were then asked to construct a graph (opposite) which plots the quality of experience that Eva has during the time span of the play. They do this using a line graph. This can be annotated if the teacher wishes.

Such graphs can be prepared by individuals, pairs or small groups and if presented on acetate for OHP or on

| **Events in Eva Smith's Life** ||
|---|---|
| 1. | 1910. Employed at Mr Birling's factory |
| 2. | Strikes for pay rise and sacked for being a trouble-maker |
| 3. | Out of work |
| 4. | Taken on at Milward's and enjoying her employment |
| 5. | Sacked from Milward's |
| 6. | Changes name to Daisy Renton |
| 7. | On the streets |
| 8. | Meets Gerald and becomes his mistress |
| 9. | Gerald leaves her |
| 10. | Meets Eric at the Palace Bar |
| 11. | Brief fling with Eric |
| 12. | Finds out she is pregnant |
| 13. | Approaches the charity where Mrs Birling is Chairperson |
| 14. | Is turned away by Mrs Birling |
| 15. | Takes her own life by drinking disinfectant which burns her insides |
| 16. | Dies a painful death April 1912 |

(My thanks are due to Coby McKeon, Assistant Headteacher at Carr Hill High School in Lancashire for this example of a 'tension graph'.)

Principle

an interactive whiteboard, the class can debate the different lines of rising or falling tension or happiness and where graphs show major differences, individuals can be asked to justify their decisions using evidence from the text.

The visual representation of events in the play will support those students who are visual learners and this format requires them to process information for understanding.

It can be used with any age group or level. One school used a 'tension graph' with an A level group studying Frankenstein who produced a "Frankometer" around three sides of the classroom to chart the emotions of Victor Frankenstein at various points of Shelley's novel.

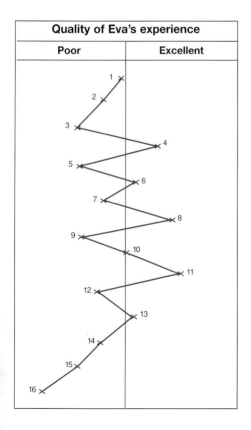

Principle

# Visual planning

Many students struggle when asked to plan extended writing essays, reports, evaluations, projects, talks or presentations. They make notes, compile information, evidence, images, data and so on but find it difficult to turn this into a formal, well-structured end product. Visual planning will help many learners in this process.

In the example that follows, the process is completed as a whole-class activity using the visual planning software *EyeWrite* on an interactive whiteboard. The same process could be undertaken by individual students or small groups on a PC or laptop.

## Stage 1: Collect information and ideas

The students, using ideas from their prior learning, initial reading or discussion, brainstorm key words which are recorded randomly on the whiteboard and then stored in the word hoard at the side. Images from clip art, department or web collections are stored at the bottom of the screen.

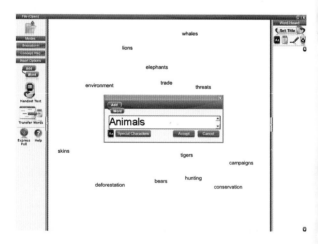

*"Teachers fortunate enough to have Promethean's Activexpression handsets can use them for the brainstorm. All learners use the keyboard on the handsets to text their ideas to the screen. Hover the mouse over each idea and it tells you who sent it."*

**Thinking and processing**

## Stage 2: Initial sort

A simple sorting exercise will help the student to begin to identify the key branches or headings. Thinking and discussion skills are being used.

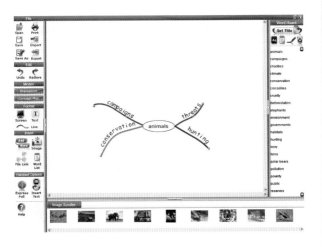

## Stage 3: Design the visual plan

The key words and images are mapped as in the example. The visual plan can also include digital camera or video clips.

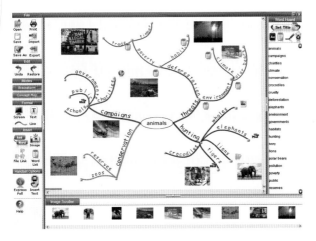

If you would like to see a free demonstration of EyeWrite[3] using the Activexpression handsets please email info@robertpowellpublications.com.

Thinking and processing

## Stage 4: Add more detailed information or notes

The students can now right click on key words and add additional information that will be used in the final product. (If students prefer, the process of adding notes can take place at Stage 3 as the map is created.)

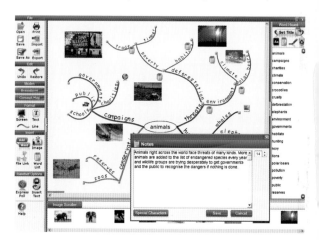

## Stage 5: writing the report, evaluation, project or essay

The visual planning software then converts the visual plan into a word processing document with the sections and paragraphs shown along with the notes made earlier. (See opposite.)

*"Those learners, of all ages, who find the planning and structuring of writing or speaking difficult (e.g. planning a talk in Modern Foreign Languages), will find that the visual plan helps them enormously. The main headings of the talk in the example given are - Threats, Hunting, Conservation and Campaigns. These become the chapters or sections of the writing or speaking. The smaller branches on each of the main headings – environment, deforestation etc. – become the sub-paragraphs in each section.*

*This visual structure is replicated once the visual map is converted to text. Learners will benefit from this type of planning and be able to plot their own work visually before a new piece of writing or before planning a talk or presentation."*

**Thinking and processing**

### animals

**threats**
Animals right across the world face threats of many kinds. More animals are added to the list of endangered species every year and wildlife groups are trying desperately to get governments and the public to recognise the dangers if nothing is done.

environment
Changes to the environment are one of the major concerns for wildlife experts. Global warming is predicted to have a huge imapct upon both human and animal life with some parts of the world due to be under water within 100 years.

climate
Changes to the climate are having an impact upon wildlife in many parts of the world. The thickness of the ice in the polar caps is reported to be getting thinner and thinner every decade and this will almost certainly result in the extiction of animals such as Polar Bears that depend upon the ice.

polar bears
Polar Bears depend upon the ice to hunt for seal. If the ice disappears then they will find it almost impossible to eat because in the water seals swim much faster than Polar Bears and will get away very easily if attacked.

deforestation
One of the major problems facing animals is the loss of habitat and in some areas of the world rapid deforestation is the biggest cause of animal decline.

habitats
Habitat is critical to the survival of animals. The habitat provides the shelter from predators and if this is lost there will be a long-term decline in that species. Habitat also provides the food that sustains the life of many

he Word document still has to be developed into a
:port or essay, but for those students who lack
 onfidence or skills in planning and organising
 xtended writing, the process provides a valuable
 atform or scaffold.

)etails of the Visual Planning software *EyeWrite* can be
 und in the Resources section on page 144.)

# Through Learning Styles

In the earlier, Personalised Learning version of this book I included a section on learning styles. Like many, I had been seduced into believing the claims of those who argued that 'research' showed that multiple intelligences and learning styles were established facts instead of just theories. Coffield, Moseley, Hall and Ecclestone (2004) published a systematic and critical review of learning styles and pedagogy in post-16 education. In a later publication (Coffield, 2008 p 32) Coffield summarises their findings:

> *"The most worrying aspect of this movement is that it appears impervious to evidence-based criticism. Our detailed and systematic review found that ... 'there is no evidence that the model is either a desirable basis for learning or the best use of investment, teacher time, initial teacher education and professional development' (Coffield et al., 2004 p 35). Put simply, it doesn't work."*

Had I studied the available research on learning styles, and the researchers found 71 different such theories, I would have been more sceptical of the claims. I regret I naively accepted the plausible ideas presented by the evangelists, but then so did many teacher education departments, the DfE, Ofsted and the now-defunct QCA.

If the research findings are accurate, and I do agree with their general conclusions, particularly with regard to their implications for teaching and learning, then many schools need to re-think their policies. I know of schools that use questionnaires to assess learning styles. Based on the results they then label students (e.g. auditory, visual or kinaesthetic) and then introduce a policy that requires teachers to plan lessons to meet these learners' various needs. In the most extreme examples, learners wear labels identifying their preferred style. This is preposterous on two counts, even if we accept the validity of the original questionnaire used to assess the styles, most of which the research found to be flawed. Firstly, if learners are weak in reading and writing, surely they need to do more of these rather than concentrating on kinaesthetic activities? Secondly, if the theory is applied, teachers in a class of 30+ will have to plan multiple activities to meet the various needs, including those who have a mixture of 'styles'. Ask teachers who teach 25 lessons a week if this is the real world and you will get an honest and abrupt response!

The debate on learning styles will, I am sure, rumble on. I would prefer to concentrate on the issue of variety in teaching and learning. I have led over 1000 training days with teachers from all sectors and have never met any professional who denies the value of a mixed economy in the classroom. Outstanding teachers use a wide range of strategies: talking and listening, group work, visual and auditory stimulus, making and doing, using ICT, role play – the list is endless. Learners love variety – just ask them.

Examples of plot and character cards from Henry V.

A good example of variety in learning is provided by the best SEN resources I have ever found - those published by Cutting Edge Publications from Cornwall. This publisher has rewritten many popular novels and plays for a readability age of eight years, adding wonderful illustrations in both the text and the playing cards that come with each pack. Many of the publications have also been recorded with sound effects onto DVD. Learners will engage with each novel or play – reading, listening, sorting cards, talking and writing at various points in the learning process. Each pack has a tremendous variety of stimuli with access being provided in a number of ways. This is not about learning styles; it is simply good practice.

**Differentiation**

# By Task

## Differentiation by task

In some classrooms teachers use twenty-question worksheets where question 1 is a 'yes' or 'no' and question 20 is a PhD. The most confident students complete all 20, the majority the first 10 and the least confident finish only 3 or 4. The quickest students never finish – they simply get 20 more! This is not differentiation. Differentiation is about ensuring that when tasks are set they provide a range of opportunities – from access for the least confident or skilled to challenge for the most confident or talented.

## Extension tasks

One of the ways to differentiate by task is to provide a basic set of questions or activities with an extension for those that work quickly or for those that need greater challenge. This approach is widely used by both teachers and by publishers of textbooks. The example below is from a Geography lesson on Weather and Climate.

---

### Weather and Climate

**Activities**
1. Describe the location of deserts around the world.
2. Identify some plants and animals that have adapted to life in the desert, and list their special features.
3. Outline a list of tips that will help people survive in hot deserts if they are lost.
4. Explain why hot deserts are found in the tropics.
5. Identify and explain how a number of different plants and animals have adapted to desert life.

**Extension**
A. Explain how the global circulation of air in the atmosphere has created hot deserts on either side of the equator.
B. Research how indigenous people like the Bushmen of the Kalahari survive in hot desert regions.

---

The key to a successful extension activity is that it requires learners to go further and deeper than in the original tasks, and can also ask them to undertake a little original research as with the Bushmen of the Kalahari.

Differentiation

## Different tasks

Another form of differentiation by task, also quite popular with teachers, is to set different tasks. For example, if in mathematics a teacher was teaching the rules of 'area', the practice questions might include tasks such as these:

---

**Calculate the area of the following shapes:**
1. A rectangle 20cm X 15cm
2. A football or hockey pitch 75m X 45m
3. A painting on the wall 1.2m X 0.75m

---

Such tasks would not challenge someone who had mastered the basic formula for the area of rectangles so confident students might be offered a different task: how many square metres of turf are needed to redo these lawns?

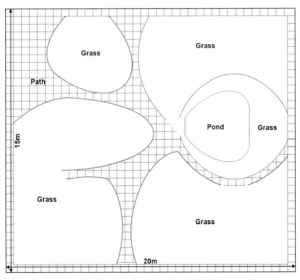

Thanks to Katie Young for this diagram

This type of task can be modified to make it more or less challenging: it might include a variety of shapes and perhaps other calculations related to the costs of laying the turf. This principle of differentiation by task can be applied to most subject areas and for most age groups.

# 'Must', 'Should', and 'Could' tasks

Another approach is to plan tasks or assignments that have a number of different degrees of challenge, ones that relate closely to the levels or to the grade criteria set out by the teacher or examination board. (This links closely to the principles on Assessment later in the handbook.) This approach is also one that can be used to integrate a range of key skills within the teaching of the subject matter.

Principle 3 of the Teaching Section (page 30) stresses the importance of key words. So, in the following example from a primary school topic in Science on the subject of Habitats, the starting point is 20 key words.

| temperature | camouflage |
|---|---|
| light | predator |
| plant | Sun |
| soil | habitat |
| consumer | shade |
| mammal | sample |
| woodland | animal |
| water | food |
| prey | pond |
| food chain | insect |

There has been some formal teaching on the subject and students have watched a video on Habitats and have done some research on Internet sites suggested by the teacher. There have been a number of whole-class discussions on the topic and some lively debate about environmental issues.

Rather than asking students to plough through a series of mundane worksheets on Habitats, the teacher has decided to ask students to complete one extended piece of writing or project to summarise their learning.

The assignment has a number of key features. It is designed:

1    to stimulate students

2    to have a clear purpose

3    to lead to a real product

4    to develop report and persuasive writing skills

5    to develop skills in research, thinking and ICT.

The learners have to process the information they already have and draw conclusions that will demonstrate their understanding of the topic itself and of the issues related to scientific investigation and evidence. This approach brings together in one piece of work Principles 2, 3 and 4 of this section on Learning.

It also addresses another key issue that was raised earlier. The 'high stakes' tests that exist at all levels cannot be dismissed while students, schools and colleges are judged on the information that the tests provide to LEAs and to parents. Such data is also very important to inspectors. They are increasingly using such data, particularly that related to value-added, in making preliminary judgements on institutions they are about to inspect.

The focus on testing may have contributed to the perceived decline in extended writing skills and the inability of many students 14-19 to plan projects, assignments, presentations and essays. Using the approach that follows regularly during the 7-14 phases as a part of the 'mixed economy' would prepare students for the challenges of more independent planning in later years, skills so valued by employers.

## You are going to learn about the relationships between living organisms in their habitat

**Your task: you are going to solve the mystery of who killed Farley Fox.**

**Background crime scene information: Fox found dead at edge of wood, not eaten. Predator may have been scared off after kill. Forensic tests show the fox had eaten that day.**

### You must

- Include in your report details of the type of habitat in which the suspected murder of Farley Fox took place.
- Describe the temperature, humidity, light levels and how these might have had an effect on how and why the murder took place.
- Suggest food chains that the fox may have been involved in that day.
- Name suspects and why they could or could not have been the killer.
- You should use at least 5 words from the topic word list.

### You should

- Describe the habitat of each plant, animal or micro organism you interview in connection with Farley Fox's death.
- Name any other organisms that your suspect has eaten, may eat or may be eaten by, to gather a solid bank of evidence. Record your investigation in an annotated food chain diagram.
- Consider all possible causes of death: accident; poison by plant or animal defences; predator; old age or disease; and decide from all the evidence you have collected who or what is the most probable suspect or cause of death. Say if the evidence is inconclusive.
- Use at least 10 words from the topic word list.

### You could

- Change the murder victim and type of habitat: for example a shark in the Pacific Ocean, or a sea lion in the Arctic. Use CD-ROM and information texts to research the other living organisms and environmental conditions for your chosen habitat.
- Use photographs to illustrate your case, to be presented in court.
- Tell the court how reliable your conclusions are and be honest if the evidence is inconclusive.
- Use most of the words from the topic word list.

**Differentiation**

The task has clear purpose from the beginning. The interest in forensic detective dramas on TV makes the 'solve the mystery' focus of the task a likely winner in terms of motivation. It also makes it clear that science can be exciting.

The 'must' section sets out the basic level of achievement expected. The least confident students who succeed at this level will actually complete a piece of work – not like in the 20-question worksheet approach.

Notice that students have to use key words in context.

Greater expectations in the 'should' section.

It is not one of those 'woolly' find out projects that led to so much unfocused project work in the 60s and 70s.

Clear guidance and prompts are included to guide the planning.

The prompts are not only helpful to students but also to support staff, librarians and parents.

Real challenge in the 'could' section. The task is real science but includes so many other skills that are valuable in both education and life.

This type of activity structure can be used in any subject or vocational course and can lead to a variety of products, not just writing: speaking, making and doing presentations, multimedia assignments and numeracy or mathematics.

The example opposite is from Business Studies, but with a few modifications it could become a handling data assignment in Mathematics or an ICT assignment for presenting graphical data. Readers should assume that the task is accompanied by sets of figures on sales and costs.

As in the Habitats example, the starting point is the key word list.

| Mean | Percentage | Significance | Turnover | Revenue |
|------|-----------|--------------|----------|---------|
| Overheads | Gross Profit | Trading | Profit and Loss Account | Net Profit |
| Expenses | Administration Expenses | Seasonal | Fluctuating | Uncertainty |
| Mean | Forecast | Expenses | Marketing | Break even |

The Business Studies example has all the differentiation features of the Habitats project but this one illustrates how easy it is in this type of assignment to incorporate the key skills that must be developed in post-16 education. A wide range of communication, numeracy, ICT and presentation skills are demanded and all in the context of the subject being studied – so important for the credibility of both teachers and students.

(Thanks to Vice Principal Designate of Sir Stanley Matthews Academy in Stoke-on-Trent, for the Business Studies example opposite.)

## Challenging able and talented students

The 'must', 'should' and 'could' approach works well for supporting some learners and challenging others. There are, of course, many approaches to challenging the most confident, and one of the best books for this is Barry Teare's *More Effective Resources for Able and Talented Children*. (See Resources section on page 144.)

You are the new Managing Director of a sports and leisure shop. The shop sells: (1) sports equipment; (2) sports and leisure clothing; (3) outdoor leisure equipment e.g. tents; (4) outdoor sports clothing.

Your task: The Board of Directors has told you that your key task is to improve sales, reduce costs and improve the profitability of the company. You are going to present a report (or a presentation) to the Board explaining the current position of the company along with your plans and forecasts.

*You must*
- Include in your report a table giving details of total monthly sales, costs of sales and overheads for the past 12 months.
- Present the figures for annual Gross and Net Profits.
- Identify the top selling ranges and those less successful.
- Use evidence to say from which area of sales it would be best to launch new products. Identify two new products that you plan to launch with a sales forecast for 12 months.
- You should use at least 5 words from the key word list.

*You should*
- Produce graphs showing monthly sales, costs of sales and overheads.
- Produce details of monthly sales for each product range with the mean sales for the year.
- Produce a pie chart that compares sales of the various product ranges
- Analyse the graphs and pie charts and explain any patterns that exist which will help the company to be more successful.
- You should use at least 10 words from the key word list.

*You could*
- Produce a spreadsheet with sales forecasts, costs of sales and overheads for your new products for the next 12 months.
- Use spreadsheet formulae to calculate Gross and Net Profit.
- Create charts/graphs to display this data.
- Use the spreadsheet and associated charts and graphs to show what would happen if the company could achieve a saving of 10% on overheads.
- Suggest how such a saving could be made.
- Use most of the words from the key word list.

# Differentiation through ICT

The ICT revolution in schools and colleges means that more and more teachers and students are able to gain access to technology that can provide real support in meeting the many and various needs of individuals. Even at the simple level, word processing, spell checkers and the 'undo' facility have made writing less threatening to those with poor literacy skills.

## Differentiation through access

Interactive whiteboard technology can offer students different access points for learning: the function of the heart; the rain cycle; the workings of an engine – all come alive in animated or video sequences. Put the same software onto a network and individuals can stop any sequence at will and see it again when they need repetition.

## Differentiation through the medium

Many students are asked to show their understanding through writing and for many this is a medium they have yet to master. ICT provides a range of media through which students can demonstrate their learning.

## Differentiation through the product

Once students have access to the technologies and the skills to use them, creativity can begin to return to classrooms. ICT provides students with a wide range of opportunities to present to others what they can do and what they know. The following table of creative ideas from John Davitt illustrates this perfectly.

The table opposite is from John Davitt's new book *New Tools for Learning, Accelerated Learning meets ICT (see Resources section on page 144 for more details).* John's analysis of current provision for ICT use in education and his vision for the future of technology are superb – the most insightful and inspirational that I have come across. It includes not only the philosophy that surely must drive schools forward but a host of brilliant ideas for making the technologies available a central part of effective and creative learning.

- Make your own daily radio news programme.

- Design, illustrate and publish your own German comic.

- Make your own history radio programme - hear it broadcast last thing on a Thursday as school finishes.

- Insert a clip of yourself into a piece of archive video footage on Home Front commentary from the war, talking about rationing, for the lunchtime video shorts competition.

- Animate a water molecule passing through a cell wall for the biology resource bank. See it used as part of a large (turbo-teaching) group lecture for students in Year 7 (visitors always welcome).

- Make your own feely bag relief map of Europe.

- Design a learning mat (an A3 placemat with pictures and text to recount the detail of a module). This could also contain individual targets to map out the learning and provide a visual and textual roadmap through it.

- In a small team put together two key animations to show key learning points that have been taught and understood, for example peristalsis, continental drift, osmosis.

- Make an animated timeline of the last century.

- Produce a 'zoomagram' of the solar system starting in outer space and ending up at the road outside the school using flick-paper animation or software such as Flash.

- Make a 3D 'feelagram' of the liver – drawn by hand, scanned on the computer, labelled, then printed out and modelled and vacuum-formed in the CDT room.

Thanks to Network Continuum Education for permission to reproduce this table.

New Tools for Learning

Accelerated learning meets ICT

**Differentiation**

One quote from John's book stands out in my mind:

> *".. the technology is powerful only when the educational purpose is strong."*

The book is a must for those keen to develop the creative use of ICT to enrich the curriculum and the learning experiences of students.

## Self-paced learning

ICT performs a major role in classrooms all over the world and will continue to do so. Individuals' needs are often met by them selecting programs which offer a range of challenge and activity, and, working alone, they progress 'at their own level and at their own pace', receiving feedback and reports to guide them in their learning. ICT is also a powerful tool in whole-class activity, with interactive whiteboards and multimedia software transforming learning and teaching experiences. But no software has yet managed to combine all of the following with 30+ learners at the same time:

- differentiation
- self-paced learning
- motivation
- 100% participation
- instant, real-time feedback.

*Not until now.*

Promethean, the world leader in response technology, has developed an amazing function for its Activexpression response handsets. Teachers are able to author sets of questions at a variety of levels (e.g. Level 1 to Level 5), requiring a range of possible responses including text or numeric input, multiple-choice, true or false or rank in order. The questions appear on the screen of the handset and learners respond at their own pace. The software can be programmed to increase the difficulty level of the question after, for example, two successful answers. So, within a minute of starting, some learners will be on Level 1, some on Level 2, some on Level 3, some on Level 4 and some on Level 5.

The whole process is recorded live on the interactive whiteboard screen with colour-coded bar charts

**Differentiation**

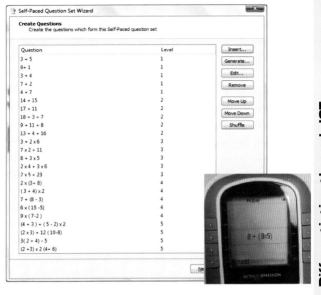

| Question | Level | |
|----------|-------|---|
| 3 + 5 | 1 | Insert... |
| 9 + 1 | 1 | Generate... |
| 3 + 4 | 1 | Edit... |
| 7 + 2 | 1 | Remove |
| 4 + 7 | 1 | |
| 14 + 15 | 2 | Move Up |
| 17 - 11 | 2 | Move Down |
| 18 - 3 + 7 | 2 | Shuffle |
| 9 + 11 + 8 | 2 | |
| 13 + 4 + 16 | 2 | |
| 3 + 2 x 6 | 3 | |
| 7 x 2 + 11 | 3 | |
| 8 + 3 x 5 | 3 | |
| 2 x 4 + 3 x 6 | 3 | |
| 7 x 5 + 23 | 3 | |
| 2 x (3+ 8) | 4 | |
| (3 + 4) x 2 | 4 | |
| 7 + (8 - 3) | 4 | |
| 6 x (15 - 5) | 4 | |
| 9 x (7 - 2) | 4 | |
| (4 + 3) + (5 - 2) x 2 | 5 | |
| (2 x 3) + 12 (10 - 8) | 5 | |
| 3(2 + 4) - 5 | 5 | |
| (2 +3) x 2 (4 + 6) | 5 | |

informing teachers of the levels at which individuals are currently working. The feedback to teachers is instant and live, allowing them to intervene when they see a student struggling with particular questions. An instant intervention can lead to quicker understanding, unlike in normal classrooms when feedback from marked work is days or even weeks after the activity. As you can see in the diagram below, teachers are able to hover over the responses of individual learners and see instantly how they responded. The whole process can be paused if the feedback on the screen indicates a question is causing widespread problems for the students.

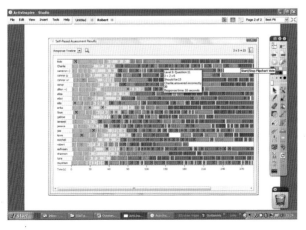

**Differentiation**

Furthermore, the software can be programmed to offer learners more than one chance to answer each question, and the live records show how often students are able to master a concept or skill when they are allowed to re-try a question without the peer pressure that exists when this is done orally in front of the class.

| Name | Response | Time |
|---|---|---|
| Bobi | 23 | 21.6 s |
| cameron ) | 23 | 10.5 s |
| Charlie | 55 | 13.0 s |
| Charlie | 55 | 10.0 s |
| Charlie | 23 | 14.5 s |
| connor g | 55 | 17.8 s |
| connor g | 55 | 13.8 s |
| connor g | 23 | 46.3 s |
| connor wl | 23 | 8.6 s |
| conor | 60 | 24.1 s |
| conor | 23 | 17.0 s |
| dillon =) | 55 | 7.7 s |
| dillon =) | 23 | 14.7 s |
| eliza | 23 | 7.7 s |
| elliot | 55 | 23.6 s |
| elliot | 23 | 16.3 s |
| ellis | 55 | 5.2 s |
| erika | 23 | 15.6 s |
| faye | 55 | 9.7 s |
| gabbie | 55 | 7.5 s |
| gabbie | 23 | 6.1 s |
| ismaeel | 55 | 6.8 s |
| ismaeel | 23 | 14.9 s |
| jessica | 55 | 4.9 s |
| jessica | 55 | 6.9 s |
| jessica | 55 | 9.3 s |
| jessica | 23 | 26.0 s |
| joe | 55 | 5.7 s |
| joe | 55 | 9.4 s |
| joe | 55 | 7.2 s |
| joe | 55 | 9.5 s |
| joe | 55 | 15.8 s |
| joe | 55 | 5.7 s |
| joe | 55 | 17.7 s |
| joe | 55 | 3.2 s |
| joe | 55 | 2.2 s |
| joe | 23 | 35.4 s |
| lewis | 55 | 21.8 s |
| lewis | 23 | 9.7 s |

In the image above, you can see how Joe understood the BIDMAS (some use BODMAS) rule on his 10th attempt but got the next question right first time. He finally understood! This opportunity would not be possible in a normal class lesson.

The exercise provides all kinds of assessment data. The teacher can study the response record of each individual learner (below), how each individual

| | Level 1 | | | Level 2 | | | Level 3 | | |
|---|---|---|---|---|---|---|---|---|---|
| | ✔ | ✘ | ⏱ | ✔ | ✘ | ⏱ | ✔ | ✘ | ⏱ |
| Angus | 10 | 2 | 0:09 | 10 | 1 | 0:13 | 10 | 2 | 0:13 |
| Anita T | 10 | 2 | 0:08 | 10 | 0 | 0:09 | 10 | 8 | 0:19 |
| Atlanta | 10 | 1 | 0:05 | 10 | 0 | 0:09 | 10 | 1 | 0:10 |
| Ben H | 10 | 3 | 0:07 | 10 | 0 | 0:04 | 10 | 5 | 0:09 |
| Courtney Lea | 10 | 0 | 0:06 | 10 | 6 | 0:14 | 10 | 14 | 0:20 |
| Elisha Heywoo | 10 | 0 | 0:04 | 10 | 0 | 0:09 | 10 | 0 | 0:06 |
| Elle H | 10 | 0 | 0:06 | 10 | 0 | 0:08 | 10 | 0 | 0:11 |
| Ellie | 10 | 1 | 0:08 | 10 | 2 | 0:09 | 10 | 1 | 0:06 |
| Elliot | 10 | 1 | 0:12 | 10 | 5 | 0:25 | 2 | 0 | 0:15 |
| Emily | 10 | 2 | 0:08 | 10 | 1 | 0:05 | 10 | 0 | 0:07 |
| Ethan | 10 | 1 | 0:10 | 10 | 1 | 0:17 | 10 | 1 | 0:15 |
| Georgia | 10 | 2 | 0:07 | 10 | 1 | 0:10 | 10 | 4 | 0:12 |
| Hassan | 10 | 0 | 0:12 | 10 | 1 | 0:12 | 7 | 6 | 0:22 |
| Hinna | 10 | 1 | 0:08 | 10 | 0 | 0:10 | 10 | 1 | 0:11 |

**Differentiation**

## Self-Paced Assessment Results

Level Summaries ▼

| Name | Level 1 ✓ | ✗ | ⏱ | Level 2 ✓ | ✗ | ⏱ | Level 3 ✓ | ✗ | ⏱ | Level 4 ✓ | ✗ | ⏱ | Level 5 ✓ | ✗ | ⏱ | ✓ | ✗ |
|---|---|---|---|---|---|---|---|---|---|---|---|---|---|---|---|---|---|
| Bobi | 4 | 1 | 0:10 | 4 | 0 | 0:09 | 4 | 0 | 0:20 | 4 | 0 | 0:11 | 0 | 0 | 0:26 | 0 | 0 |
| Charlie | 4 | 0 | 0:07 | 4 | 0 | 0:08 | 4 | 15 | 0:37 | 4 | 0 | 0:00 | 0 | 0 | 0:00 | 0 | 0 |
| cameron :) | 4 | 0 | 0:06 | 4 | 0 | 0:10 | 3 | 17 | 0:31 | 0 | 0 | 0:00 | 0 | 0 | 0:00 | 0 | 0 |
| connor g | 4 | 0 | 0:05 | 4 | 0 | 0:10 | 4 | 7 | 0:42 | 2 | 1 | 0:12 | 0 | 6 | 0:34 | | |
| connor w! | 4 | 2 | 0:06 | 4 | 0 | 0:06 | | | | | | | | | | | |
| conor | 4 | 0 | 0:09 | 4 | 0 | 0:08 | | | | | | | | | | | |
| dillon =) | 4 | 0 | 0:08 | 4 | 1 | 0:15 | | | | | | | | | | | |
| eliza | 4 | 1 | 0:09 | 4 | 0 | 0:09 | | | | | | | | | | | |
| elliot | 4 | 0 | 0:07 | 4 | 0 | 0:11 | | | | | | | | | | | |
| elis | 4 | 2 | 0:05 | 4 | 0 | 0:05 | | | | | | | | | | | |
| erika | 4 | 0 | 0:05 | 4 | 2 | 0:14 | | | | | | | | | | | |
| faye | 4 | 1 | 0:06 | 4 | 2 | 0:07 | | | | | | | | | | | |
| gabbie | 4 | 0 | 0:07 | 4 | 0 | 0:06 | | | | | | | | | | | |
| smaeel | 4 | 0 | 0:04 | 4 | 0 | 0:05 | | | | | | | | | | | |
| jessica | 4 | 0 | 0:05 | 4 | 0 | 0:05 | | | | | | | | | | | |
| joe | 4 | 3 | 0:10 | 4 | 0 | 0:07 | | | | | | | | | | | |
| lewis | 4 | 0 | 0:08 | 4 | 0 | 0:11 | | | | | | | | | | | |
| mitchell | 4 | 0 | 0:09 | 4 | 0 | 0:09 | 4 | 12 | 0:35 | 0 | 2 | 0:06 | 0 | 0 | 0:17 | | |
| robert | 4 | 1 | 0:04 | 4 | 0 | 0:06 | 4 | 1 | 0:07 | 4 | 0 | 0:10 | 3 | 0 | 0:17 | 0 | |
| safwaan | 4 | 0 | 0:07 | 4 | 1 | 0:07 | 3 | 25 | 0:46 | 0 | 0 | 0:00 | 0 | 0 | 0:00 | 0 | |
| shannon | 4 | 0 | 0:05 | 4 | 0 | 0:11 | 4 | 0 | 0:20 | 0 | 0 | 0:12 | 1 | 3 | 0:30 | 0 | |
| tyra | 4 | 0 | 0:06 | 4 | 0 | 0:08 | 4 | 1 | 0:12 | 0 | 0 | 0:05 | 0 | 8 | 0:39 | 0 | |
| zaysham | 4 | 0 | 0:06 | 4 | 0 | 0:04 | 2 | 37 | 0:50 | 0 | 0 | 0:00 | 0 | 0 | 0:00 | 0 | |

Question 14: 2 x 4 + 3 x 6
Answered incorrectly in 29 seconds: 66 should be: 26
Question 13: 8 + 3 x 5
Answered incorrectly in 17 seconds: 55 should be: 23
Question 13: 8 + 3 x 5
Answered incorrectly in 13 seconds: 55 should be: 23
Question 11: 3 + 2 x 6
Answered incorrectly in 10 seconds: 36 should be: 15
Question 11: 3 + 2 x 6
Answered incorrectly in 14 seconds: 36 should be: 15
Question 11: 3 + 2 x 6
Answered incorrectly in 31 seconds: 30 should be: 15
Question 11: 3 + 2 x 6
Answered incorrectly in 10 seconds: 30 should be: 15

responded to a particular question (above) and the class response to each question. All can be saved and printed for the purpose of record keeping.

Seeing Self-Paced Learning in action is a revelation. I have never before seen a class where there was 100% participation, total engagement, sustained concentration and not a wasted second in an activity that lasted nearly 15 minutes.

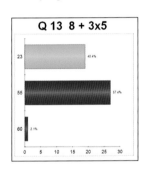

Q 13 8 + 3x5

The teacher and teaching assistant were fully occupied, prompting learners in real time as mistakes were made, feedback coming from the screen as it all happened. This is why Promethean now refer to this process as Real Time Personalised Instruction (RTPI).

If you would like to see self-paced learning in action with a real class in your school, please email info@robertpowellpublications.com ref self-paced learning. This will not cost the school anything provided the enquiry is a genuine one.

# Basic skills

Basic and key skills are the building blocks for most learning and teachers should find ways to integrate them in their teaching and learning programmes whenever possible.

## Integrating basic skills in the planning of tasks

Principle 3 in Teaching (starting on page 30) emphasised the need to identify and build the key vocabulary. If this process is in place then the development of skills can now be further enhanced in the planning of tasks. This will work where the purpose of the task is to develop understanding, not necessarily test it (see page 72 for the full explanation on this).

Look at the two versions of the worksheet below.

*Basic Skill:* ***Literacy (writing)***

---

### Version 1. Typical worksheet

1 Where in the body do you find cholesterol?
2 What kinds of foods contribute to the build-up of cholesterol in the body?
3 Name one kind of illness that can occur if you eat too much fatty food.
4 Name three types of food that can provide energy.

---

- The worksheet encourages short response answers (e.g. 'in the arteries').
- There is little scope for the development of writing skills.
- It is easy to respond without real understanding.
- It will do little to motivate learners.

Now look at the second version.

## Version 2. Incorporates literacy

You are a healthy-eating consultant. A client has written the following letter:

> Dear Consultant
> My doctor has told me that my cholesterol levels are too high. I do not know what this means or what I should do. Can you help?

Reply to the letter using and explaining the following words:

> Cholesterol, arteries, heart disease, fibre, vitamins, balanced diet, saturated fats, exercise, meats, carbohydrates, protein.

- This task now requires students to compose and write a formal letter.
- Students have to process their knowledge of the subject and explain their guidance to the client.
- The task will cover the same ground as the original worksheet but now incorporates literacy skills (e.g. sentence work, connectives).
- The task leads to a real product that can be used as part of a display or web page.
- The key words on display in the classroom and practised through activities like Blockbusters (see page 32) have to be used in a real context.
- Scaffolding and connectives can also be used here to support the learners.

The first example shows how easy it is to adapt an existing worksheet to develop literacy skills. It can also be used to create a speaking and writing task.

*Outstanding Learning*

## Version 1. Typical worksheet

1 Where in the body do you find cholesterol?
2 What kinds of foods contribute to the build up of cholesterol in the body?
3 Name one kind of illness that can occur if you eat too much fatty food.
4 Name three types of food that can provide energy.

## Version 2. Speaking and writing skills

You are a healthy-eating consultant. A client calls you on the telephone with the following query:

"I have been told by my doctor that my cholesterol levels are too high. I do not know what this means or what to do. Can you help?"

Working with a partner, write the script for the conversation that follows and then be prepared to perform it in front of the class. You must include the following words in your conversation:

Cholesterol, arteries, heart disease, fibre, vitamins, balanced diet, saturated fats, exercise, meats, carbohydrates, protein.

● The task now requires students to write a script in dialogue form.

● Students have to process their knowledge of the subject and explain their guidance to the client.

● The task will cover the same ground as the original worksheet but now incorporates writing and speaking skills.

● The task leads to a real product that can be recorded and used as part of a web page.

*Basic skill: **Numeracy***

The same activity can easily be adapted to incorporate numeracy. An extension to the previous task might be included.

---

### Extension task

During the conversation the client explains that s/he is a pensioner on a fixed income and cannot afford to spend too much on food.

You offer to post an example of a balanced diet for one week with a table showing prices of the chosen foods.

Create this diet sheet, listing the prices of foods and setting them out in a table.

---

- All kinds of challenging scenarios might be offered.
- Numeracy here is in the context of the course.
- Spreadsheets might be used.

Other products are possible, of course: the formal letter could be replaced by *persuasive* writing because the client is reluctant to consider a more balanced diet.

# Key skills

In many schools and colleges, particularly post-16, teachers are required to develop a range of key skills. Creative approaches are also productive here.

*Key Skills:*
**ICT, writing, numeracy, design, group work.**
The activity set out below involves the use of small groups and would work well as part of a community/ citizenship project delivered through the curriculum.

You are the editors of a community newsletter. Obesity is on the increase amongst young people.

You have been asked to produce a Newsletter 'Special' on Healthy Eating.

Your newsletter can include:

- Articles on obesity and heart disease and their causes.
- Features on approaches to healthy living including diet and exercise.
- Photographs, data, graphs and appropriate images.
- A 'please help' problem page with letters from readers and the replies.
- Case studies and/or interviews with members of the public or health specialists or doctors.
- An editorial/opinion section.
- Fun page with, for example, crosswords, word searches and/or a quiz.
- Adverts from sponsors e.g. health foods, exercise programmes or equipment.

Your newsletter will be produced and delivered freely to the local community.

Although the topic lends itself to courses like Health and Social Care, the actual approach could be used in any subject and the key skills required can be amended to suit individuals' needs; this is *differentiation* in action:

- The task might be changed to the creation of a website rather than a newsletter.

- The key features might be modified to include video clips or radio interviews.

- The tasks might have greater emphasis on any of the key skills e.g. numeracy.

- Within a school it might become a cross-curricular project (Food, English, Art, ICT, Maths, PE, Science, MFL, and Citizenship). It might involve community partners.

- It might be possible for students to enter elements of the work as portfolio evidence or coursework.

Once the creativity of teachers is released then most things become possible.

Integration is important. Tasks that advance the key skills but do nothing for the subject or vocational course are unlikely to be popular with either students or teachers; time is too precious to waste on what both will see as 'peripheral' activities.

But the principle can apply in many situations. The outline tasks overleaf will illustrate this. All of them would have additional guidance in the form of 'must', 'should', and 'could' (see page 88) and could be adapted for a range of skills.

**Geography**: river valleys

You have been given the job of planning a two-day canoe trip, down a river of your choice, to highlight how the river and valley changes.

*Your task*: you will need to investigate how a river and its valley change as you go from the source towards the mouth. You will then need to plan and write an interesting and informative programme for the trip.

**History**: 1918 Germany

You are a History expert employed to advise a film producer working on a 1-hour documentary on Germany in 1918.

*Your task*: Germany faced many problems in 1918 immediately after the First World War. Identify and prioritise the key issues and then decide how long to devote to each issue in the hour.

**Science**: inheritance and selection

You are the owner of a Stud breeding horse. You are going to report on selective breeding.

*Your task*: you have been asked to prepare a formal report for racehorse owners who want to know how to breed a Derby-winning racehorse.

**Physical Education**: muscular system

You are going to learn about how the muscular system works.

*Your task*: design part of a revision website for the PE department. The topic is the muscular system. The website should help students in their revision.

**Engineering**: mechanisms

You are going to learn about mechanical systems.

*Your task*: write a short article, explaining to a group of primary pupils how three simple mechanisms work to make life easier. Choose three e.g. bike gears, nail clippers, a winch or a wheelbarrow (or others).

**Hair and Beaut**y: training manual

You are going to produce a training manual for new students.

*Your task*: using images and text produce a storyboard for the treatment of a client (hair or beauty). Use technical terms whenever possible.

**Construction**: building regulations

You are going to learn about regulations relating to foundations.

*Your task*: You are a builder in the early stages of constructing a five-storey apartment block. You have just put in the foundations when the building inspector arrives. Write the script of the conversation you have.

**Art**: pattern

You are going to learn how to do a screen print.

*Your task*: write the instruction manual for a silk screen package. It has to help newcomers to this craft. They would like the instructions to be done as a series of bullet points with images.

**Music**: music of the Caribbean

You are going to learn about music of the Caribbean.

*Your task*: You have been asked to explain, in the programme for a local music festival, the background to a piece of reggae music you composed, which is to be performed at the event.

**Performing Arts and Drama**: Blood Brothers

You are going to explore the relationship between Edward Lyons and Michael Johnstone in Blood Brothers.

*Your task*: You are a police officer. After questioning Mrs Lyons and Mrs Johnstone, you have sufficient evidence to write up the background to the case to produce a report for the investigation into the shooting.

**Hospitality and Food**: organising a banquet

Produce a quotation for a potential client for a banquet for 250 people.

*Your task*: The client does not know exactly what she wants so you have to set out in a formal letter a range of choices for the format, the menu, the entertainment and the venue. Include spreadsheets and menus.

**Religious Education**: attitudes to animals

You are going to learn about views on the issue of animal rights.

*Your task*: Three of your friends, a Muslim, a Christian and a humanist, have been arrested at a demonstration outside a department store selling real fur coats. Prepare a statement in their defence on behalf of the organisation. This statement will be read out in Court.

# Outstanding...

| Principle | The Challenge |
|---|---|
| **1.** The key purpose of assessment is to promote learning and should actively involve all students. | Assessment activity is increasingly important. Teachers, students and other partners in education should be absolutely clear on the distinction between assessment of and assessment for learning and the complementary roles they play in raising achievement. |
| **2.** Assessment criteria should be shared with and understood by all individual students. | Teachers should ensure that all students understand the criteria that will be used to make judgements on their performance. Learners should also be able to recognise features of a task or assignment that will lead to a higher standard, grade or mark. |
| **3.** Students should be able to assess their own work and the work of others. | Peer and self assessment can equip students with the skills and confidence to plan their own work in line with targets for improvement. |
| **4.** Marking should provide *feedback* that celebrates achievement and identifies targets for improvement (*feedforward*). | Marks or grades do not inform students of how they might build on, develop or change their future work to make progress. Focused marking with clear targets for future action by individual students is more likely to lead to a positive response than a policy of correcting everything. |

# Assessment

Assessment

# Definitions

This handbook is focused on outstanding practice in the classroom and as such will look at those aspects of assessment that can support individuals' needs within learning and teaching. The use of data will be examined briefly, but the major emphasis will be on *assessment for learning* in the classroom and how it can be used to help to support teachers and their students to maximise achievement.

## Definitions

Assessment for Learning (AfL) is not new. Ruth Sutton's brilliant book *Assessment for Learning*, published in 1995, is based on her earlier publication *Assessment: a Framework for Teachers* published in 1991.

The topic may not be new but it has seen a massive surge of interest in recent years, mainly due to the work of the Assessment Reform Group and the publications *Inside the Black Box* and *Working inside the Black Box* by Professors Paul Black, Dylan Wiliam and others at Kings College, London. The DfES in England has also recognised the contribution that AfL can make to its campaign to raise levels of achievement in schools, and a number of initiatives are now underway in post-16 institutions.

The best definition of Assessment for Learning I have read is:

> *"Assessment for learning is...the process of seeking and interpreting evidence for use by learners and their teachers to decide where the learners are in their learning, where they need to go and how best to get there."*

(Assessment for Learning. 10 Principles. Assessment Reform Group 2002)

The definition comes from an excellent research-based leaflet from the Assessment Reform Group that sets out 10 key principles for AfL, all of which are examined in more detail in this book. The Assessment Reform Group believes that AfL should:

1   Be part of effective planning of teaching and learning

2   Focus on how students learn

3   Be recognised as central to classroom practice

4   Be regarded as a key professional skill for teachers

5   Be sensitive and constructive and take account of the emotional response to assessment

6   Take account of the importance of learner motivation

7   Promote commitment to shared learning goals and assessment criteria

8   Ensure that learners receive constructive guidance on how to improve

9   Develop skills of reflection and self-assessment

10  Recognise the full range of achievement of all learners.

Definitions, by their very nature, can be misunderstood, misinterpreted and even used mischievously on occasions to defend or attack a position, so schools and colleges must ensure that definitions used in policies are accompanied with concrete examples if they are to result in the development of real practice in the classroom. Such models follow in the remainder of this section on assessment. A range of examples follow.

# AfL and Learning and Teaching

## The link between **AfL** and Learning and Teaching

Schools that seek to develop assessment for learning projects will quickly learn that many of the strategies that fall broadly within the AfL umbrella cannot be fully implemented without teachers ensuring that key aspects of learning and teaching accompany the work on assessment.

1 **Independent learning**. AfL requires students to be actively involved in peer and self assessment.

   *If too much teaching is dominated by the teacher, students become passive and unresponsive to AfL.*

2 **Effective tasks and assignments**. In AfL, students are able to set personal targets in terms of levels or grades because they understand the assessment criteria and know what they have to do to reach their goals.

   *Some worksheets or assignments are closed, low level or lack differentiation and are so inflexible that they prevent individual target-setting.*

3 **Feedback** is a critical aspect of successful AfL, often involving dialogue with individuals or small groups.

   *In large classes, feedback with individuals or small groups will be difficult to achieve unless students generally are capable of working independently while the teacher is engaged in the dialogue. For teachers to be able to work uninterrupted in this way, learning tasks must be well planned and students must be clear about the tasks that have been set. For this to be achieved, classroom management strategies need to be in place and systems of support in place (e.g. support groups).*

4 **Classroom displays**. Assessment criteria need to be clear if students are to set personal targets or to evaluate their own work or the work of others. Models of practice are essential if they are going to be able to interpret the complex language used by examination boards. In practical lessons models can be demonstrated, but for other activities examples need to be displayed or accessed through ICT.

*Some teachers, particularly in Further Education, spend their time moving from room to room carrying their blue plastic boxes containing all the resources they need for that lesson. Displays will be impossible and ICT access is often physically some distance away.*

5 **Agenda for Teaching, Learning and Assessment**. The motivation, self-esteem and confidence of students is central to AfL. Without a 'can-do' philosophy, many students will not take advantage of the benefits AfL can bring to learning and teaching. Motivation and self-esteem are usually enhanced if teachers are successful in engaging students and encouraging their participation in a non-threatening and supportive environment. Clear purpose, pace, encouragement and positive feedback are all key characteristics of such classrooms.

*Some lessons lack purpose, planning is poor, engagement and motivation are absent and poor behaviour and disruption can follow. Staff development, peer observation and teamwork will help to bring about the changes needed. For this to happen, senior managers must put outstanding teaching, learning and assessment at the top of the agenda. Other policies, for example those related to behaviour and pastoral support, must complement those on teaching, learning and assessment.*

# Using Data

The theme of this book is outstanding teaching, learning and assessment so references to data are only included in relation to classroom practice. This is not to suggest that other uses of data are somehow less important. Indeed, there are numerous examples of schools and colleges using data to drive up standards, to raise expectations and to monitor the progress of learners.

- **Refining national curriculum levels**. Some teachers will divide a level into 3 or use a decimal system to show whether students are high, middle or low within a level.

- **Using data to predict and to set targets**. (E.g. the Autumn package in schools in England.) This will include the policy of making predictions with added 'challenge'.

- **Involving pastoral tutors in academic monitoring/tracking**. Tutors will use data provided by subject specialists to monitor and chart students' progress across a range of courses, bringing in other data on attendance etc. to paint the big picture, often involving parents.

- **Involving students in the process of using data**. In the best systems students are fully involved in the process of analysing the data and of setting personal targets.

- **Using a range of information, including standardised tests**. Some schools take published data and add CATs and MIDYIS/YELLIS/ALIS scores to give predicted outcomes at Key Stage 3, GCSE and A level.

- **Using outside agencies**. The Fischer Family Trust can provide, as part of a project working through LEAs, a range of analyses and data, including estimates for individual students' likely performance based upon progress. This process is similar to the ones used by the DfES with its contextual value-added data (CVA).

(For more detailed advice on data see *Making Pupil Data Powerful* by Maggie Pringle and Tony Cobb. Resources section page 144.) Thanks to Maggie Pringle for advice on these pages on Data.

Purpose of assessment

# Using data to promote learning

The pressure on schools and colleges to collect and analyse data of all kinds has increased in recent years. This pressure will intensify if inspectors continue to place great emphasis on data, particularly CVA data, in the production of pre-inspection hypotheses.

However the data is collected and however it is analysed, it should have one overriding function: to promote learning. The use of data should involve teachers and students in a dialogue designed to raise aspirations and expectations; dialogue such as:

> *"Students of your prior attainment generally achieve x in this subject. However, some students last year achieved x + 1. What do we have to do to help you achieve x + 1?"*

Such a simple dialogue has two desirable outcomes:

- It moves the debate quickly from data analysis to action related to learning, teaching, skills and motivation.
- It places the students' learning and day-to-day experiences at the heart of the process.
- It gives teachers and support staff a clear agenda for improving the performance of individuals and in the long run the performance of the team or department.
- It demonstrates clearly the need to bring teaching, learning and assessment into one coherent and consistent policy.

So, the data that is so important in the defining and monitoring of progress can only raise achievement if the information and insight it provides is used by teachers and students to improve the range and quality of the teaching and learning experiences. As Joan Sallis once pointed out so succinctly, *"weighing pigs don't fatten them"*.

There are many examples that could show how feedback from assessment data can be used to promote learning. The one overleaf makes use of exciting new technology to do this.

# Data from electronic feedback

In the section on outstanding learning, I explained how Activexpression response handsets can be used to improve motivation and levels of participation. The example that follows shows how these response handsets, used with exciting software, can:

- engage all learners
- secure 100% participation
- be used as a starter or plenary, and...
- provide rich and powerful data to support learning.

### The Race Game AfL (*Assessment for learning*)

The Race Game brings computer games to the classroom primarily as a learning and assessment activity. The fact that learners love playing the game is a bonus!

The Race Game is a race around a motor-racing circuit using Promethean's Activote or Activexpression response handsets (it will not work with other response systems). It works with any make of interactive whiteboard or on a normal screen with a digital projector. Learners are each allocated a car or they can play collaboratively in teams with up to 32 cars on the grid. The race starts and every 8 seconds or so a multiple-choice question appears on the screen.

Learners use their Activote or Activexpression handsets to respond and the race screen returns. Those who selected the correct answer see their cars accelerate; those who were wrong see their cars slow down. Cars overtake just as in a normal motor race and it is wonderful to see a car starting at the back of the grid storming to the front to the delight of the player.

The Race Game Editor which comes with the software allows teachers to create questions for any subject and for any age. The questions can be text, image or sound/music.

There are three databases of published questions ready for use with the software: 20,000 questions for mathematics from Level 3 to Level 7, 15,000 grammar and spelling questions from Level 3 to Level 7 and 6,000 science questions from Level 3 to Level 8.

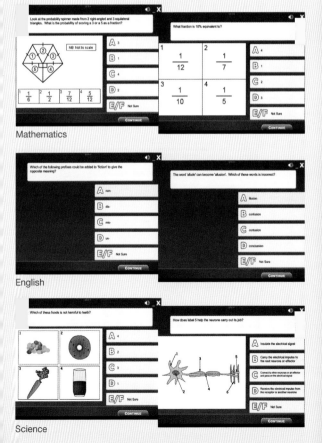

Mathematics

English

Science

**Purpose of assessment**

The Editor also allows users to edit existing questions or mix and match questions from different levels from the databases.

*Feedback data from the Race Game*

The Race is not just a game. The electronic handsets record all responses during the game and immediately provide the teacher with rich data on the performance of each and every individual.

## ANALYSIS

| Select Test | Question 6 | Question 7 | Question 8 | Question 9 | Question 10 | Totals | Percentage | Avg. Response | User |
|---|---|---|---|---|---|---|---|---|---|
| 268375 15/08/2008 | D | B | D | C | D | 6/10 | 60% | -0.64s | Blair,Tony |
| 99618 15/08/2008 | D | A | D | C | A | 7/10 | 70% | -0.48s | Boudicca,Queen |
| 271616 15/08/2008 | D | C | a | B | C | 5/10 | 50% | -0.77s | Charlton,Bobby |
| 204864 15/08/2008 | D | A | D | B | C | 6/10 | 60% | -0.47s | Coe,Sebastian |
| 232697 15/08/2008 | D | B | D | A | C | 7/10 | 70% | -0.70s | Dors,Diana |
| 21605 14/08/2008 | D | A | D | B | A | 4/10 | 40% | -0.37s | Duck,Donald |
| | D | B | D | C | C | 7/10 | 70% | -0.69s | King,Billie-Jean |
| | D | C | D | C | C | 8/10 | 80% | -0.49s | Mouse,Mickey |
| | D | A | D | C | A | 6/10 | 60% | -0.55s | Nadal,Rafa |
| | D | A | D | C | A | 7/10 | 70% | -0.73s | Ratcliffe,Paula |

**Analyse Questions**   **Export to Excel**

The feedback also provides a percentage figure for each question which enables the teacher to identify questions which caused problems for the class.

| Select Test | | | | | | | | | |
|---|---|---|---|---|---|---|---|---|---|
| 268375 15/08/2008 | Coe,Sebastian | C | A | D | B | B | D | C | D |
| 99618 15/08/2008 | Dors,Diana | C | A | D | B | A | D | B | D |
| 271616 15/08/2008 | Duck,Donald | B | A | D | A | B | D | A | D |
| 204864 15/08/2008 | King,Billie-Jean | C | A | D | B | A | D | B | D |
| 232697 15/08/2008 | Mouse,Mickey | C | A | D | B | A | D | D | D |
| 21605 14/08/2008 | Nadal,Rafa | C | A | D | A | A | D | A | A |
| | Ratcliffe,Paula | C | A | D | A | A | D | B | D |
| | Thatcher,Margaret | C | A | D | B | B | D | D | D |
| | Victoria,Queen | B | A | D | B | A | D | D | D |
| | | 75% | 0% | 100% | 67% | 75% | 100% | 17% | 83% |

**Analyse Questions**   **Export to Excel**

The data allows the teacher to use the game as an integral part of the lesson because the software provides analysis, question by question, of how learners responded. Individuals who answered correctly can explain their solution to the class or can help others in a peer coaching activity. All results can be saved to Excel.

Principle

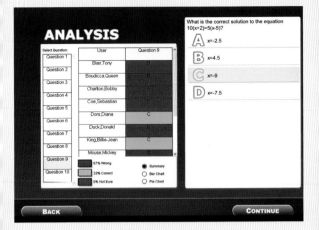

Feedback being used instantly to correct misunderstanding is a powerful example of *Assessment for Learning*. Electronic feedback makes this possible – it would be days or even weeks if the questions were assessed manually and the important information on the numbers getting each question right or wrong would be impossible without the aid of electronic devices. Formative assessment, we must remember, is only formative if the information or data results in some kind of intervention. In the example above the Race Game used as a starter provides information which can shape the remainder of the lesson, and used as a plenary it can help the teacher plan future lessons so it is clearly a good example of formative assessment in action.

Readers who would like more information on the Race Game AfL can see a video of a class using it by visiting www.robertpowellpublications.com or by logging into YouTube http://www.youtube.com/watch?v=dH6HgDTfo44.

Readers who would like a demonstration of the Race Game and/or Activexpression response handsets with a real class should email

info@robertpowellpublications.com

and a visit from one of our team to your school will be arranged. There is no charge for this demonstration provided the enquiry is a genuine one and that the visit is agreed by senior staff.

Principle

# Sharing assessment criteria

## Published criteria

Most teachers will make use of the assessment criteria published by examining boards, awarding bodies and government departments. Copying these for students, particularly post-16, will be common practice. In vocational courses most students will be given folders where the units of work are set out with clear descriptors on how each unit will be accredited, and the criteria used to judge performance, levels or grades.

A problem that most teachers will be familiar with is the tendency of some accreditation bodies to obscure the meaning of the criteria with the use of technical jargon, primarily because the guidance is aimed at teachers, not the students.

In vocational courses, many of which are designed around coursework and portfolios, the criteria need to be targeted at students who need access in order to study independently. Yet even here some of the language used creates a barrier for those who are not confident with language. This is why many teachers choose to interpret the criteria for their students.

## Interpreting criteria

One approach that works well for post-16 students is for the teacher to explain and illustrate the performance/level/grade descriptors with examples while students discuss the content, ask questions and then make notes. If students place the examples on a page directly opposite the published criteria in a ring binder, as in the example opposite, they should be able to use the criteria with more confidence, reading the descriptors while looking at the examples.

### Induction activities

Once the assessment folder has been prepared with examples, as in the example, teachers can divide the class into small groups and ask each group to use the published documents to produce a presentation to explain the criteria while other groups act as 'critical friends', asking questions or seeking clarification when

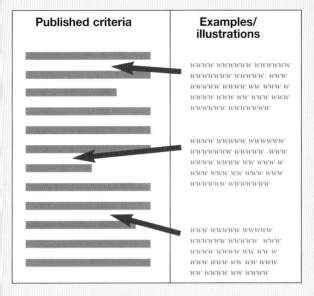

| Published criteria | Examples/illustrations |

necessary. This process is effective because teaching others is an effective way to learn. This induction process is best done unit by unit, so that as a new topic or assignment begins, students study the guidance and understand from the beginning how their completed work will be judged and what they have to do to achieve their personal targets.

## Translating the criteria

Many teachers choose to translate the assessment or performance criteria into documents that are accessible to the students themselves.

I worked for an afternoon with a team of Learning Support teachers in a school in Knowsley keen to translate the English Level Descriptors into an accessible form.

They wanted learners to be actively involved in setting personal targets, but the language of the descriptors was inaccessible. For example, the QCA document for Level 2 in 'writing', because its target audience is teachers, includes phrases like:

*"...sometimes demarcated by capital letters and full stops....simple, monosyllabic words are ...the alternative is phonetically plausible."*

This is Level 2, and while some primary age or lower secondary children might, with guidance, cope with this language, it will be inaccessible to most and totally incomprehensible to young people with learning difficulties.

Furthermore, each paragraph contains a number of different skills that taken together constitute progress at that level. Young people do not learn in that way, however. A target that says *try to attain Level 2 by Christmas…* is not helpful to learners with low self-esteem. It is much better to break down the skills into very small 'chunks' so that daily progress can be made. The illustration below is a copy of what The Learning Support Team produced in our workshop.

| A1 | A2 | A3 | A4 |
|---|---|---|---|
| I use I, not i. | I use a full stop at the end of a sentence. | I can use a comma. | I can use letter at t of a sent |
| **A5** | **A6** | **A7** | **A8** |
| I can use a capital letter for a proper name. | I can use a question mark. | I can write a sentence. | I write lines. |
| **A9** | **A10** | **A11** | **A12** |
| I start sentences with different words. | I use my ruler. | I can use connecting words. | I can do writing |
| **A13** | **A14** | **A15** | **A16** |
| I put my date and heading at the | I can keep my writing straight | I can keep my letters the same | I bring a pencil, rul |

My thanks to Knowsley St Edmund Arrowsmith Catholic High School for permission to use this example.

This personal log is not presented as a set of level descriptors but as a set of 20 individual skills that might be used by learners, their Learning Support Assistants and teachers to provide evidence that certain levels have been reached. But the students do not think in terms of levels, which is a teacher term linked to national assessments, but in terms of what they can do; this is related to learning rather than to assessment. I will return to this example later in the section on personal targets.

The same approach has been followed for behaviour targets. Once again, massive targets such as 'improve your behaviour' are daunting for many young people.

Shared criteria

Individual, specific sets of behaviours are easier to deal with.

| B1 | B2 | B3 | B4 |
|---|---|---|---|
| I arrive on time. | I go straight to my place and sit down. | I put my hand up when I want to speak. | I listen to instructio |
| **B5** | **B6** | **B7** | **B8** |
| I sit where I am told to sit. | I can sit quietly for 5 minutes. | I do not wander around. | I do not others w |
| **B9** | **B10** | **B11** | **B12** |
| I show respect to others. | I follow classroom rules. | I admit it when I have done something wrong. | I say sorr I am wro |
| **B13** | **B14** | **B15** | **B16** |
| I do not make fun of (skit) others. | I thank others when they help | I keep my temper. | I do not s school. |

Another example of translating criteria is set out below. In this example from a Yorkshire school, the criteria are given to all students for their folders and large posters are also displayed. When new assignments begin, the assessment criteria are used in the thinking and planning that goes on.

| | HISTORY ATTAINMENT TARGET LE | | |
|---|---|---|---|
| Level | Content & Chronology | Causes & Consequences | Interpretin |
| 5 | c) You know **detailed facts** and have a **deeper knowledge** about British & other History.<br>d) You use this knowledge to make links between past societies and periods | You describe detailed causes and results of events and changes, but you also **make links between them**, showing how one cause led to another. | You know so **specific exa** how events, changes hav represented ways. **You e** this happene |
| 6 | You can **describe different** societies and periods from British and other history, and make **clear links within and across** periods. | You can **examine causes and results** in detail, and **analyse** them, looking at **links** and **types** and **importance**. | You can desc different interp and **begin to** why and ho come about. |
| 7 | c) You show an outline of factual knowledge about British and other History, and detailed knowledge about various periods.<br>d) You **use this to analyse relationships** | You can analyse causes and results – **grouping** them together & **linking** them, identifying different **types, prioritising** them. | You can ex and why dif interpretations come about |

Thanks to Alison Munro and the History Department of Aston Comprehensive in Rotherham for the use of this example.

The next phase for such guidance is to use it for peer and self evaluation (see pages 128 and 132).

# Student-led criteria

There will be many occasions when teachers are working with a group of students when a particular topic or focus does not lend itself to assessment in terms of published levels or grades. This does not mean, however, that the perceived benefits of AfL – motivation, participation, engagement and understanding – cannot apply. Indeed they can. The approach where students themselves define the criteria will be equally valuable.

---

### Example 1

### Focus: effective presentations using ICT

**Task**: to plan a presentation to promote a new product to an imaginary sales conference.

**Stage 1**. In support groups (see page 68) students are asked to identify the features of a good sales presentation. Key prompts on planning sheet to scaffold the discussion.

**Stage 2**. Plenary: chairperson for each group reports back and after discussion from class, agreement is sought on features of effective presentation. These are recorded, displayed and distributed to each group.

**Stage 3**. Each group plans its own presentation, using the agreed criteria to guide them.

**Stage 4**. Each group in turn gives its presentation while other groups use the criteria to assess it.

**Stage 5**. Feedback is given with questions, as each group has its presentation assessed publicly.

**Stage 6**. Class revisits criteria and amends them in the light of experience.

---

In the second example the teacher uses role play in order to highlight the importance of clear criteria and reliable evidence in any debate where opinions and emotions are strong.

## Example 2

### Focus: Using evidence to make judgements

**Task**: to present and evaluate the evidence for or against a proposed new shopping centre development.

**Stage 1**. Class is divided into groups and allocated one of 4 roles: (1) the developers, (2) existing businesses, (3) members of the public and (4) homeowners near the proposed development.

**Stage 2**. All groups now draw up their criteria, reasons or evidence for accepting or rejecting the proposed development. Guidance and scaffolding sheets made available along with necessary access to resources.

**Stage 3**. Each group in turn presents its set of criteria to an imaginary public 'forum' (a Town Planner might have been invited) and takes questions.

**Stage 4**. The Town Planner (or teacher) now invites each group to assess the good and the weak points or criteria presented by other groups.

**Stage 5**. In the class plenary students are asked to agree which evidence was (a) strong and convincing, (b) reasonable and (c) no more than opinion.

In both of these scenarios, and teachers will think of many others, students have been fully involved in assessing the work of their peers. In both they are engaged from the beginning and I have no doubt that the lessons they will learn about quality, evidence and the nature of assessment will be longer lasting than being 'told'.

# Modelling

Another example of translating criteria is set out below. In this example from a London school, the criteria are given to all students for their folders and large posters are also displayed. When new coursework assignments begin, the assessment criteria are used in the planning that goes on. This is just one section of the criteria.

---

**Knowledge & Application of Language (/5)**

To get 2 out of 5 you **must**:
- Use some appropriate vocabulary
- Use simple sentences
- Attempt to use key phrases ('Il y a...', 'il n'y a pas...','j'aime... parce que...'etc.
- Show some use of adjectives and adverbs
- Use simple subordinate clauses ('J'aime... parce que...'/ 'Quand j'ai du temps libre, j'aime aller.....'etc.)

**To get 3 out of 5 you** should:
- Use a range of appropriate vocabulary and structures
- Use simple sentences and syntax well
- Use adjectives, adverbs and genders (masculine, feminine and plural) regularly
- Use linking subordinates (puis / après ca / ensuite / donc etc.)
- Manipulate the stimulus (i.e. use it as a guide to create your own work).

**To get 4 or 5 out of 5 you** could:
- Use a wide range of vocabulary and structure to suit the task
- Use a variety of structures and idioms
- Express and justify opinions
- Use complex structures with confidence e.g. Pronouns
  ( mon m

---

Thanks to Whitecliffe Sports College for permission to use this.

They also did practice coursework units in an induction phase and displayed extracts from pieces of work on a notice board.

Shared criteria

> *Mon père travaille dans une usine..*

This will get 2 marks because it uses a simple sentence.

> *Mon père travaille tous les jours dans une petite usine familiale.*

This sentence is worth 3 marks because it uses adjectives and adverbs.

> *Mon père travaille tous les jours dans une petite usine familiale, mais moi j'aimerais travailler dans un bureau après mes examens.*

This will get 4 marks because it uses adjectives and adverbs but also expresses opinions.

Modelling can take many forms:

**Improve the writing**

reached  perceived  engraved

When she got to the castle she saw the words written over the door

forced  crept

"Be bold, be bold!" She pushed the door open and went in. It was

gazed

dark and spooky. She held up her lantern and looked around

nervously. In one corner there was a young lady hanging by the neck,

scream

in another corner there was a head that seemed to say, "Help! Help!"

She looked under the table and there was more blood on the floor.

prised open

Then she saw a box on the table. She opened the box and saw a

piece

peace of hair tied with ribbon.

- Visual examples on display boards
- Worked examples on the whiteboard as in the example above
- Annotated work on websites for reference
- Practical demonstrations by teachers or other students.

The key purpose is to allow learners to view the criteria, to see them applied in real examples and then be able to use the immortal words of Alan Bleasdale's famous character from Boys from the Black Stuff, Yosser Hughes:

## *"I can do that."*

Shared criteria

# Peer assessment

Black and Wiliam are clear that both peer and self assessment are valuable in promoting learning, but they believe from their research that skills in peer assessment should be developed first. Two key ground rules need to be established before self assessment is used:

1    Establish from the outset with all concerned that the purpose of self assessment is to help individuals to have a deeper understanding of assessment and what constitutes progress and success. This will enable them eventually to plan their own work to meet targets.

2    Create a safe, non-threatening and supportive environment by emphasising that no destructive or sarcastic comments will be expected or tolerated. The concept of 'critical friends' may be helpful in explaining this process.

Peer assessment will not be effective until the assessment criteria have been shared and discussed as examined earlier in this chapter. This can also include student-led criteria (pages 120 and 124).

It is best in the early days of peer assessment to use work from an *anonymous* student. Coursework or projects from previous students might be used here and it is also a good idea early on to restrict the scope of the assessment to a short section of a project if it is in written format. Do not make the task too daunting or there is a danger of negative feelings colouring the experience.

There are a number of ways of proceeding. This is just one:

---

### Example 1

1 Organise the class into groups of no more than 3 or 4 students.

2 Photocopy or display the work to be assessed.

3 Ensure that each group has a copy of the criteria for success and that they have been discussed and understood.

4 Explain whether the assessment must lead to a judgement on levels or grades achieved or whether the judgements are to be qualitative in nature e.g. 'what might be done to improve'.

5 Ask each group to assess the work using the criteria. Emphasis that evidence from the text or product must be identified that justifies the comment, suggestion, level or grade.

6 The teacher will be fully involved but working at small group level, cajoling, questioning, praising and prompting.

7 Each group now presents its findings, taking questions from other groups. Debate is encouraged but with an emphasis on friendly discourse rather than full frontal attack.

---

The benefits of this anonymous approach is that students learn the skills of assessing work in collaboration without any of the stress associated with assessing the work of people they know.

Once students have been exposed to the non-threatening assessment of anonymous work then teachers can extend it to peer assessment.

## The language of peer assessment

The ground rules described at the beginning will need to be firmly in place but teachers will need to provide guidance also on the language of assessment.

The street language of some students when asked 'What do you think of it so far?" will be "cool" or "rubbish". They need to be equipped with appropriate language so it is worth investing some time in this training and even having a writing frame or poster with appropriate phrases:

*"I like that but have you thought of…"*

*"The best part of the…is when you…"*

*"This conclusion does not meet the criteria for a higher grade because…"*

*"I think that next time you ought to…"*

*"The reason this is awarded a high mark is because…"*

The kinds of phrases used will depend upon the age of the students, the subject, the level and the confidence and skills of those involved.

## Parents

Peer marking is one of the ways of using these approaches to develop assessment skills. In schools it is worth investing some time explaining the approach to parents – reducing the marking load of teachers is not the prime purpose!

## Peer assessment possibilities

There are so many ways of using peer assessment it is probably better to provide a brief description of a wide range of approaches than just a few in detail.

1  Asking learning partners to make helpful suggestions on each other's drafts, with a balance towards the positive. E.g. three aspects that they like and one that they think can be improved.

2  Asking learning partners to draw in pencil a smiley face next to parts of a partner's work that they like and a glum face next to parts that

might be improved. The author of the work has to work out why the faces are there!

3  Ask learners to mark their partners' answers to questions by putting a cross next to errors but without identifying what is wrong. The authors then have to correct the answers while in dialogue with their partners.

Peer assessment of understanding, not just of completed work, can also be very effective. Question Time (see page 42) is one example of this in action.

4  Ask partners to set questions for each other to test understanding or for revision purposes. The answers must always be prepared by the questioner first!

5  Ask learners to provide answers; their partners have to work out the questions! E.g. in Psychology the answer is Skinner. What was the question?

6  Ask students to examine past examination papers and select a question that they would like to revise. They work out their own version of this question for other students to do in a mock test. The real learning comes from the fact that the student setting the test has to produce not only the question but the answers and mark scheme. They make use of examiners' reports to help them do this. (Brilliant at Advanced Level/Highers/Level 3.)

# Self assessment

Once learners have been regularly exposed to the skills of peer assessment they should be ready to engage in positive self reflection and self assessment. The purpose and its link to effective learning must be clear:

- to learners
- to teachers and assistants
- to parents.

The purpose of self assessment is to enable learners to make judgements on their own work with the prime purpose of (a) recognising and celebrating success and progress and (b) identifying avenues for progress or improvement. All learners should aim to improve on their previous best and in this respect it matters not one jot what other students have or have not achieved.

Self assessment at its best is the simple process of doing what the Assessment Reform Group on page 110 referred to in their definition of assessment for learning. It enables learners to know where they are in their learning, "where they need to go and how best to get there".

A clear understanding of the criteria for success will enable this to happen and that will only happen if learners are exposed to regular peer and self assessment experiences that are seen by all as natural extensions to the learning and teaching and not a one-off, occasional exercise.

One example of self assessment being a natural part of learning and teaching is shown below. The two pages shown are the front and back of a single A4 personal record sheet. The process is simple:

1. Record learning aims along with personal targets from previous assessment.
2. Record ideas, modifications etc. that come as a result of formative feedback from the teacher.
3. Student reads summative assessment, talks to teacher if necessary and then records self-evaluation.
4. Student selects and records targets to feed forward to next assignment.

132

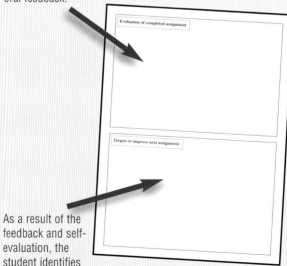

**Personal Record Sheet**

Name _____  Form/Subject _____
Topic _____  Date started _____

Learning aims of the assignment, including personal targets

Guidance, agreements, changes etc.

Evaluation of completed assignment

Targets to improve next assignment

Clear *learning aims* recorded by student in line with policy of clear understanding purpose of tasks.

Dialogue with teacher involving *feedback* during the assignment is recorded by the student along with any changes that result.

Self-evaluation conducted after receiving written and/or oral feedback.

As a result of the feedback and self-evaluation, the student identifies targets for improvement. These targets become one of the aims in the next assignment.

Peer and self assessment

# Written feedback

Teachers in all phases of education are faced with enormous demands in terms of the marking and assessment of students' work. A simple set of statistics can illustrate this point.

---

### Example of marking load

Teacher: Main grade teacher of English in comprehensive school.

Teaches full timetable (ages 11-18) 200 + students per week.

Each student produces on average the equivalent of 2 hours' work for marking or assessment.

Total hours per week spent on marking the 2 hours' work of each student:

- **5 minutes average per student**        **16.6 hours weekly**
- **7 minutes average per student**        **23.3 hours weekly**
- **10 minutes average per student**       **33.3 hours weekly**

---

It does not need me to point out that this kind of marking load is unsustainable and remember, this is simply the number of hours spent marking work, and does not include time spent in planning lessons or resources.

Assessment policies in schools and colleges must protect teachers from unnecessary marking loads by stating clearly the purposes of marking. This will then allow teachers to be more focused, particularly in relation to *written feedback*.

Written feedback must have three overriding aims:

1. To enable the teacher to celebrate the work and achievements of students in relation to the learning objectives that were set.

2. To identify the next steps that students might take in order to consolidate or to improve their performance in relation to the assessment criteria.

3. To provide information or data that will enable students, parents and pastoral tutors to monitor learners' progress against standards, criteria or personal targets.

If one accepts these three principles and the issue of marking load then it is clear that teachers will be unable to fulfil all three aims with each and every piece of work produced by students. It is clear, therefore, that:

- Some marking will have to be cursory with the primary purpose of saying to students "*I've looked at your work; thank you for completing it*".

- Some marking will be done by peers or by students themselves.

- Some assessment will be done as oral feedback to individuals, groups or the whole class (see page 138).

- Some will be *detailed written feedback* and will include praise and guidance from teachers on specific steps that might be taken to consolidate or to improve performance.

- Some marking will focus on levels, grades or marks based on the explicit standards set out by the course or the teacher. Feedback may not always be used here.

Assessment policies, shared with students and with parents, need to be explicit on these issues. Efforts must be made to avoid the criticism by parents that 'they no longer correct work".

*Detailed written feedback*

There are many ways in which detailed written feedback can promote learning. The table below will illustrate some of them:

| Type of written feedback | Examples |
|---|---|
| **A.** Praise or confirmation | I was pleased with the way that you...You reached Level 5 because you were able to... |
| **B.** Encouraging or seeking greater focus or development | So far so good. You have shown me.... Now you need to go further and... |
| **C.** Correction or explanation | You have misunderstood this point. The reason why.... |
| **D.** Challenging or redirecting | All your comments are accurate and well made. To achieve a Distinction, however, you would need to.... |
| **E.** Seeking explanation | Can you please explain to me:<br>1. How....<br>2. Why... |
| **F.** Asking for reflection or self-evaluation | I want you to ask yourself the following questions:<br>If ....then why......how...where else.... |

There are a number of key points to emphasise when developing a policy for written feedback.

1   *The comments should relate to the stated
    learning aims.*
    There is little point in focusing feedback on
    *presentation* of data if the learning aims were
    related to *analysis*. Attempts to mark or correct
    everything will usually lead to students learning
    nothing from the feedback.

2   *Critical comments should be expressed carefully*.
    Demoralised students are unlikely to respond
    positively even if the criticism is valid.
    Constructive (not destructive) criticism with clear
    guidance for ways forward is more likely to lead
    to improvements.

3   *Time should be found to act upon the guidance.*
    If the feedback requires the student to do
    something, as in E or F opposite, little will
    happen unless both teachers and students
    expect it to be done, and time is found for this
    to happen.

4   *There should be a clear expectation that learners
    will read and respond to written feedback.* The
    evidence from Black, Wiliam et al. (see
    Resources section on page 144) is that marks
    and grades can act as a disincentive and that
    grades, rather than the comments, become the
    focus for students - *"What did you get?"*

5   *Teachers should recognise that some feedback
    will be ineffective in written form and that
    dialogue is better.*
    A "please talk to me about this" comment in the
    margin followed by an individual or small group
    tutorial will be more effective with some students
    and/or with some kinds of complex issues.

# Oral feedback

## Feedback to whole class or individuals

Oral feedback is a wide-ranging concept. In the best whole-class lessons, interaction between teachers and students is high and teachers are constantly offering valuable instant feedback on learners' contributions. All of the instant oral feedback described below can also apply to interaction with individuals in the busy classroom.

> ### Whole-class or individual instant feedback
> *Can you elaborate on that…?*
> *That's one example. Can anyone give me another..?*
> *We need evidence. How do we know…?*
> *Is there an alternative solution that…?*
> *The learning aim says… Can anyone explain what…?*

A more formal approach is the whole-class review, particularly useful on the completion of projects and assignments. (See also Assessment Review on page 58.)

> ### Whole class review
> *Tell us, Louise, why you chose that method for…*
> *Chin, your idea of … was brilliant. Tell us how it helped to…*
> *A high grade response requires students to… Can someone tell the class how you managed to achieve that?*
> *Many of you found…difficult. Can someone explain how you overcame this?*

Such whole-class reviews are useful to both teachers and students:

1   For students it is a chance to consolidate understanding.

2 It will help some students to identify areas of concern.

3 It provides teachers with the feedback that helps them to evaluate the success of the teaching.

## Small group feedback

Much of the oral feedback described for whole-class work can also apply to the interaction with small groups, although the involvement of individuals will obviously be greater and their capacity to listen and remember feedback is enhanced from the whole-class situation.

Oral feedback through a small group tutorial is particularly useful for classes where confidence and skills levels vary enormously. (The same tutorial can be held with individuals, but it is more time consuming and many students will feel more comfortable in the safety of the group.

### Small group tutorial

In this situation teachers will offer feedback through a dialogue with groups of students selected for a variety of reasons including:

1. They all faced similar problems or misunderstandings with the assessed work.
2. They all share similar skills levels (e.g. literacy).
3. They have worked on similar projects.
4. They are all 'coasting' students needing challenge.
5. They are a 'support group' (see page 68) that work well together.

The focus for the tutorial can be:

- To give feedback on completed work or on plans for future work.
- To assess understanding or progress in learning.
- To motivate students through high-quality, personalised interaction.
- To ensure that the feedback is turned into targets (see page 140 on feedforward).

Feedback and feedforward

# Feedforward

---

**An important fact**

Teachers who spend 12 hours a week in term time assessing work (conservative estimate) will, after 20 years in the profession, have given up just over a year of their lives to this practice.

---

## The challenge

Feedback of one kind or another is not new, and readers will not be surprised by the fact above. Such devotion must be worth the effort, and in terms of written feedback I am not sure that it is.

Too often teachers spend hours correcting and analysing students' work, adding comments, suggestions and words of praise. They return the assignments to the students only to be met with a chorus of "What did you get?" from around the classroom. If the assignments are coursework they will often be collected by the teacher for safe storage. Twenty hours of teacher time is now in the filing cabinet!

If the hours spent offering written feedback is to be worth the time taken then feedback must lead to action; it must promote learning. If not, then marking is being done for the parents, for the headteacher or principal, for the sake of the policy or for inspectors, but not for the sake of the learners.

This is where the concept of *feedforward*, a term first used by Ruth Sutton, is so important. It is very simple; *feedback* from the teachers identifies the next steps for progression or improvement. *Feedforward* is the action taken by learners.

# Feedforward Example 1

This is another extract from the personal log record sheet shown on page 120. (This is a higher level example.)

| C1 I can use paragraphs. 😊 | C2 I can use speech marks. | C3 I can use a colon. | C4 I can write a conclusion. |
|---|---|---|---|
| C5 I can explain my ideas with reasons. | C6 I can write a letter. | C7 I can use adjectives. 😊 | C8 I can use adverbs. |

If this log is used by both teacher and teaching assistant then the skills can become targets at the bottom of a piece of work as in the example below.

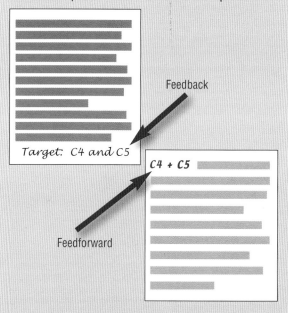

Feedback

Target: C4 and C5

C4 + C5

Feedforward

Students simply feedforward the targets to the top corner of the new piece of work. If the skills log is displayed or placed in folders, there is no need to use words, just C4 and C5. Putting them here acts as a reminder to both teacher and learner (and parents). When students master the skills, the 'smiley face' stickers are placed onto the log as in the example above. This is in essence an individual education plan for basic skills.

## Example 2

If the criteria are shared with students in user-friendly format as in this History example below, then targets can be set as the final stage of the written feedback:

| | HISTORY ATTAINMENT TARGET LE | | |
|---|---|---|---|
| Level | Content & Chronology | Causes & Consequences | Interpreting |
| 5 | c) You know **detailed facts** and have a **deeper knowledge** about British & other History. <br> d) You use this knowledge to make links between past societies and periods. | You describe detailed causes and results of events and changes, but you also **make links between them**, showing how one cause led to another. | You know so **specific exa** how events, p changes hav represented i ways. **You ex** this happene |
| 6 | You can **describe different** societies and periods from British and other history, and make **clear links within and across** periods. | You can **examine causes and results** in detail, and **analyse** them, looking at links and **types** and **importance**. | You can desc different interp and **begin to** why and how come about. |
| 7 | c) You show an outline of factual knowledge about British and other History, and detailed knowledge about various periods. <br> d) You use this to analyse relationships between different features, linking knowledge of different periods and places. E.g.: Women in different times. | You can analyse causes and results – **grouping** them together & **linking** them, identifying different **types, prioritising** them. | You can expla and why differe interpretations come about. |
| 8 | You use **detailed and outline knowledge** to analyse relationships between different features both within and across periods. | Your explanations of causes & results also include a wider **historical context**, possibly referring to similar events in different places & periods. | You can analys explain differe interpretations are beginning **evaluate them** their strengths weaknesses. |
| Excep | You show **extensive and detailed** factual knowledge, which you use to analyse | Your explanations & analysis of causes and | You can make balanced judg |

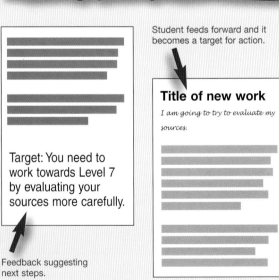

[Feedback block]
Target: You need to work towards Level 7 by evaluating your sources more carefully.

Feedback suggesting next steps.

Student feeds forward and it becomes a target for action.

### Title of new work
*I am going to try to evaluate my sources.*

Personal Logs (see also page 62 in the Teaching section).

*Example 3 Personal Logs*
Some teachers adopt a quality rather than quantity approach to marking with more detailed but less frequent feedback. They complement this with a half-termly review with individuals or small groups. During these reviews students record agreements/targets in their personal logs. One example of a personal record sheet suitable for major projects or assignments is shown on page 133 in the section on self-evaluation, and another for younger pupils is on page 62. A third example is below.

## Example 3
The personal log can be pages allocated at the back of an exercise book or a page in a student planner. Such planners are widely used in schools and contain timetables, key dates, homework pages, study skills advice and other important information. (Some have a Show Me board back cover – a brilliant way of saving time when using show-me techniques.)

The review page for an individual subject might look like this:

| Date | Science Target or agreement | Action |
|------|------------------------------|--------|
| 10 January | Discussed my habit of drawing conclusions without referring to the evidence. Have agreed to try to include more evidence in next practical write-up. | Did this on 15 January. Teacher pleased |
| 6 March | My write-ups have improved but I need to recognise a wider range of variables in my analysis if I am to achieve higher grades. | My report on 18 March did this well. |
| 5 May | | |

# Resources

p13     *Classroom Management* by Philip Waterhouse, Network Continuum Education www.continuumbooks.com

p21     EyeWrite³ visual planning software www.robertpowellpublications.com. (See on YouTube "Robert Powell EyeWrite")

p35     Blockbusters. Robert Powell Publications. www.robertpowellpublications.com

p48     Activexpression. For more information or a free demonstration in your school email info@robertpowellpublications.com ref Activexpression

p54     Dominoes. Robert Powell Publications. www.robertpowellpublications.com

p61     Promethean response handsets Activote and Activexpression. For more information or a free demonstration in your school please email info@robertpowellpublications.com

p84     Coffield F, Moseley D, Hall E and Ecclestone K (2004). *Learning styles and pedagogy in post-16 learning: a critical review*. London: Learning and Skills Research Centre, Learning and Skills Development Agency.

p84     Coffield F (2008). Just suppose teaching and learning became the first priority.... London. Learning and Skills Network.

p85     Cutting Edge Publications 01208 872 337. www.cuttingedgepublications.com

p92     *More Resources for Able and Talented Children* by Barry Teare, Network Continuum Education www.continuumbooks.com

p94     *New Tools for Learning* by John Davitt, Network Continuum Education www.continuumbooks.com

p110     *Assessment for Learning* by Ruth Sutton, available by emailing sutton.ruth@gmail.com

p110     Inside the Black Box and Working inside the Black Box www.nfer-nelson.co.uk

p114     *Making Pupil Data Powerful* Maggie Pringle & Tony Cobb www.networkcontinuum.co.uk For consultancy on data contact Maggie Pringle at maggie.pringle@tinyworld.co.uk

p116     The Race Game AfL Robert Powell Publications Ltd www.robertpowellpublications.com